MALAYAN EMERGENCY

TRIUMPH OF THE RUNNING DOGS 1948–1960

GERRY VAN TONDER

Pen & Sword
MILITARY

For my very dear friend Captain Russell Fulton RAR (Rtd)
who is an inspiration to so many

First published in Great Britain in 2017 by
PEN AND SWORD MILITARY
an imprint of
Pen and Sword Books Ltd
47 Church Street
Barnsley
South Yorkshire S70 2AS

Copyright © Gerry van Tonder, 2017

ISBN 978 1 52670 786 4

Typeset by Aura Technology and Software Services, India
Maps, drawings and militaria in the colour section by Colonel Dudley Wall
Printed and bound in Malta by Gutenberg Press Ltd

Pen & Sword Books Ltd incorporates the imprints of Pen & Sword
Archaeology, Atlas, Aviation, Battleground, Discovery, Family History, History, Maritime, Military,
Naval, Politics, Railways, Select, Social History, Transport, True Crime, Claymore Press, Frontline Books,
Leo Cooper, Praetorian Press, Remember When, Seaforth Publishing and Wharncliffe.

For a complete list of Pen and Sword titles please contact
Pen and Sword Books Limited
47 Church Street, Barnsley, South Yorkshire, S70 2AS, England
email: enquiries@pen-and-sword.co.uk
website: www.pen-and-sword.co.uk

CONTENTS

TIMELINE 1946–1960

1930	Malayan Communist Party (MCP) formed.
8 December 1941	Japan invades Malaya.
16 February 1942	Allies surrender at Singapore.
4 September 1945	Japanese surrender at Penang.
1 December 1945	Malayan People's Anti-Japanese Army (MPAJA) disbanded by the British Military Administration (BMA).
12 June 1948	The government bans trade unions after months of fomenting labour unrest.
16 June 1948	Three European planters are murdered by Communists in Perak State.
18 June 1948	Britain declares a state of emergency in Malaya.
24 June 1948	A state of emergency is also declared in Singapore at the tip of the Malayan Peninsula.
23 July 1948	MCP banned, resulting in the party militants forming the Malayan People's Anti-British Army (MPABA).
1 February 1949	The MPABA changes its name to Malayan People's Liberation Army (MPLA).
September 1949–February 1950	MPLA carry out an average of seventeen road and rail ambushes a month.
Mid-1950	Rural population moved into collective 'New Villages'.
March 1950–September 1950	Road and rail ambushes by the MPLA increase to an average of fifty-six a month.
June 1951	Operation Starvation introduced to restrict food movement.
July 1955	Malaya's first general election sees Tunku Abdul Rahman become chief minister. A partial amnesty is declared.
17 October 1955	Government representatives hold the first of three meetings with the MCP at Klian Intan.
24 December 1955	The MCP releases an eight-point programme, which includes a cessation of hostilities, the termination of emergency regulations and a demand for political reform.
29 December 1955	Talks at Baling break down as the two parties fail to agree on the future legal status of the MCP.
8 February 1956	Unsuccessful amnesty scrapped.
2 April 1956	Rahman refuses to resume talks with the MCP.

April 1957	Hor Lung, MPLA commander of southern operations, is bribed to surrender.
July 1957	Sixty per cent of Malaya is declared essentially clear of insurgents – White Area – and emergency regulations lifted.
August 1957	Kuala Lumpur declared a White Area.
31 August 1957	Malaya is granted independence from Britain, with Rahman the first prime minister.
31 July 1960	The emergency is declared officially over, but emergency regulations remain in place along the Thai border.

HRH The Duke of Edinburgh in Malaya on Merdeka Day, 31 August 1957. (Courtesy Rhodesian African Rifles Regimental Association (UK))

INTRODUCTION

'We honour Europe for its great culture. But the world is something bigger than Europe. Asia counts in world affairs, and it will count much more tomorrow than it does today.' Addressing the United Nations' General Assembly in Paris on 3 November 1948, India's first prime minister, Pandit Nehru, warned the world, adding:

> Asia, till recently, was largely a prey to Imperial domination. A great part of it is now free. But it is an astonishing thing that any country should venture still to hold forth this doctrine of colonialism.
>
> There will be active struggle against this doctrine. We who have struggled against it have committed ourselves to the freedom of all colonies. Many of these territories are neighbours of ours, and it is a narrow way of looking at it if any Power thinks they can continue to maintain directly or indirectly their colonial rule.
>
> If the peoples prepare for war, and in existing circumstances, it is difficult to say that people should not prepare to defend themselves, they must have clean hands.

The ink still wet on the 1945 instruments of surrender, the emergence of regional political and ideological dogma across the globe again threatened international stability. As the so-called Four-Power victors increasingly bickered over ownership of the defeated Germany, burgeoning nationalist movements in British and French overseas territories became far more active and vociferous in their demands for self-determination.

While Joseph Stalin was uncompromisingly intent on Soviet Communist expansionism in Europe, Mao Zedong was basking in the success of his Communist revolution in China. Chairman Mao desired to be the champion of the 'oppressed masses', espousing the formation of people's liberation movements in the European colonies. Red China and Russia would provide the instruments of insurrection: ideological indoctrination and war materiel – extremely attractive to nationalists pressing for self-government and independence.

In Southeast Asia, Japan had convincingly shown that white invincibility was a myth. The very British-armed anti-Japanese resistance movements, dominated by Chinese Communists, now turned their backs on their European masters. The transition to self-determination was relatively peaceful in Burma, but prolonged and bloody struggles ensued in the Dutch East Indies (Indonesia) and French Indochina (Vietnam, Cambodia and Laos).

The sudden proliferation of nationalist movements amongst her territories saw the still war-crippled Britain trying to save an imploding empire – liberal pressure at home added to the problem. Flashpoints of armed dissent appeared across the legacy that was Pax Britannica – Malaya, Kenya, Cyprus, Borneo, Palestine, Suez, Aden.

From the eighteenth century, Britain had set up trading establishments in Penang on the west coast of the Malaya peninsula, and on 1 May 1791, the Union Flag was raised at Penang for the first time. By the late nineteenth century, a far greater need was felt to secure the peninsula as a source of raw materials. In 1819, Sir Stamford Raffles founded Singapore – described as

战士最爱读毛主席的书

Chinese People's Liberation propaganda poster.

the ancient maritime capital of the Malays – as a British colony on the southern tip of the archipelago, deserving 'its attention to the commercial and political interests of our country'.

Early in 1826, the British press was calling it the 'prosperous state of Singapore'. Within three months of Raffles taking possession of Singapore on behalf of the Crown, the population had risen from 150 – of whom 30 were Chinese – to 3,000. The estimated 1825 population was 15,000, which included more than 3,000 Chinese.

The Bath Chronicle and Weekly Gazette of 12 January 1826, reported:

By the latest accounts it appears that capital was daily flowing in; that ten or twelve mercantile houses had been established by Europeans, and as many by Chinese, Arabians, Indians, Armenians, etc; but that the principal part of the trade and manufacturers, as well as the agriculture of the island, was in the hands of the Chinese, who also composed a large proportion of the population; that ship-building had commenced; that the banks of the river would admit vessels of 500 tons being launched; and that an active and valuable commerce in teak timber was springing up with Siam ... [amounting in] ... 1825 [to] not less than 20,000,000 dollars.

In the same year, Britain established the administrative entity known as the Straits Settlements, incorporating Penang, Singapore, and the recently acquired Malacca from the Dutch.

For the next forty years, the Straits Settlements were answerable to the East India Company, based in Calcutta, India. In 1867, the Colonial Office in London assumed control over a largely

Rubber plantation. (Courtesy John Anderson)

independent colony, and it was only in 1946 that the Straits Settlements were absorbed into the greater Malaya Union.

It was, however, only fifty years after the establishment of a settlement at Singapore, that Britain started to show serious interest in the Malay Peninsula proper. Up until early in the twentieth century, long-term leases were being secured for large areas of land in Malaya for purposes of seeking tin concessions, or planning to grow plantation crops like tea, tapioca and coffee. The demand for land rose sharply when companies formed in Britain began to look for land for rubber plantations, which, by 1940, had spread to over 2.1 million acres.

The Great Depression was disastrous to both tin and rubber production. In 1932, in London, rubber fetched one-hundredth of the top 1910 price. Malaya's exports earnings dropped by 73 per cent. The colonial office imposed strict restrictions on output in an attempt to resuscitate global prices. The outcome was mass lay-offs, and the repossession of smallholders' properties that did not have the same level of capital as the British companies to weather the recession.

The largely rural populace had already been identified in 1928 as being a target ripe for anti-British Communist propaganda. The *Nottingham Evening Post* of 14 August 1928, carried this report:

A number of remarkable documents containing principles for the conduct of Communist propaganda in Malaya have been brought to light in the trial of a Chinese committed for being in possession of seditious literature.

DANGER OF COMMUNIST PROPAGANDA

Country Already at War

Mr Frank Norvall, Director-General of the British Commonwealth section of the English Speaking Union, said yesterday that in some respects the country was already at war.

The relationship between Britain, the Dominions, and the United States of America, he said, had because of the 'cold war' greater significance than if we were really living in peace.

Communists throughout the world knew very well that if they divided Britain, the Dominions, and the United States from one another they would have won the 'cold war'. They had been trying their hardest to persuade Americans that they were being tricked into Imperialistic adventures in then Middle East and South-East Asia on the tail of Britain and France, and they had been trying to persuade us that only the danger of a war arose from the aggression of the Wall Street capitalists in America, and that the United States was trying to make us cannon-fodder for a third world war.

'We should not underestimate the danger which this sort of propaganda can do,' he said. The very fact that Britain for ten years now had been taking huge loans and grants from Canada and the United States, and always seemed to be living in a period of dollar crises, inevitably made some British people irritated with America. And on the other side of the Atlantic they were apt to wonder if it would ever end.

Those were the sort of things of which Communist propaganda could take advantage. For that reason it seemed exceedingly important that we should take active steps to create understanding between Britain, the Dominions and the United States. That was where the English Speaking Union came in.

(*The Scotsman*, Thursday, 1 June 1950)

One of them contains the following passage:

"You must rise up quickly, gather your strength, inspect your troops, use your sword and pistol, put an end to the efforts of the militarists, and overthrow the murderous policy of British imperialism. Establish a Soviet Government of labourers, peasants, and soldiers. We must unite all Malays, Klings, and Indians, and rise up. Long live the success of the world revolution."

The outbreak of hostilities in Europe in 1939 did much to stimulate Malaya's struggling economy. Tin mines, which had been operating at half capacity, were 'now operating at full capacity to meet the world demand for the metal'. Rubber production was also boosted significantly by an Anglo-American barter agreement 'under which Great Britain supplies the United States with rubber in exchange for cotton'. Thousands of unemployed and destitute, retrenched mine and rubber plantation workers were taken back on 'to ensure continued production of essential war materials'.

In January 1940, 'widespread strikes' occurred amongst Chinese industrial workers, demanding increased wages. Communist societies, described as 'very active', were believed to be responsible for fomenting civil unrest. In March, an enormous quantity of Communist pamphlets, manifestos, posters, cartoons and propaganda sheets were seized during a raid of the General Labour Union in Singapore. Three ethnic Chinese were jailed for 'sedition and membership of illegal societies'.

Malayan National Liberation Army, armed wing of the Malayan Communist Party.

In a dramatic and ironic turn of events, in December 1941, the British Malaya administration endorsed a new manifesto of the proscribed Malayan branch of the Chinese Communist party. The Malaya Department of Information gave full publicity to the document, which set out its agenda to be 'generally mobilized and armed ... to turn each street, lane, mine, village and rubber estate into a bulwark for the defence of our land. We will fight to the last drop of our blood in defence of Malaya'.

The administration had suddenly found an unlikely bed partner to combat the Japanese, but this would come at a price. It was an unwritten alliance of convenience that came from the same stable of exigency as that of Chamberlain and Hitler, von Ribbentrop and Molotov, and the Allies and Stalin.

In November 1945, British Secretary of State for War, Jack Lawson, was questioned by the Communist MP for West Fife, Willian Gallacher, as to why the Malayan Communist Party, 'which led the resistance to Japanese occupation forces in Malaya, was still an illegal organisation'.

Lawson submitted a written reply:

The Communist party was not recognised as a legal organisation under the local law as it stood immediately before the Japanese occupation, and the general policy of the military administration is to respect the previous laws and customs as far as practicable. But no one in Malaya is being persecuted for political views, and any arrests have been confined to those persons, regardless of political creed, who have broken the regulations for the maintenance of law and order. The cooperation of the Communist party has, in fact, been sought in the maintenance of good order.

(*Dundee Courier*, Thursday, 8 November 1945)

A year later, anthropologist and founder of *Mass Observation*, Tom Harrisson, put in writing his assessment of the ethnic Chinese in Malaya. Based on his long stay in the region, Harrisson contended that widespread Chinese culture in the east dated back to 'the beginning of native history'. Unlike other ethnic groups, the Chinese remained true to their ethnic origins, seldom adopting the foreign country in which they lived. According to Harrisson, not only do the itinerant Chinese work hard to accumulate wealth and go back home, but 'industry is also implicit in their philosophy of social interdependence, centred around the family group and filial devotion'.

There was an aversion to issuing Malayan passports to Chinese who essentially remained nationals of China, whether Nationalist or Communist. The indigenous Malays welcomed the large numbers of industrious Chinese tackling jobs that they despised, but when they aspired to political office, it was felt that they became a 'threat to the Malay's traditional control and political dominance'.

When the Malay sultans rejected Whitehall' s proposals for a Malayan Union in 1946, the powerful and well-organised Communist party clamoured for greater recognition of the part they played in the future of the Far East. Successive attempts by the British to devolve greater political and administrative independence to a union of Malay states and islands were also shunned.

At first light on Saturday, 10 April 1948, British army troops and Malayan police conducted an 'anti-bandit' operation into an area of North Perak, on the border with Siam. Intelligence

An MCP Communist terrorist with an Australian-made 9mm Owen sub-machine gun.
(Courtesy Brigadier John 'Digger' Essex-Clark)

sources had indicated that up to 400 'armed guerrillas' had established themselves in the border jungles between the two countries. Subversion was found to be total. The guerrillas had formed a government in the area and were extorting taxes from the people. Levels of

BANDIT WAR IN MALAYA

Divided Voices Still Speaking

With moon-cakes instead of hot-cross buns and chocolate eggs, this weekend has been for the Chinese a festival similar to Easter, and tomorrow will begin the lantern festival for the children.

The authorities in Malaya have been trying to make propaganda out of this and have dropped thousands of leaflets over bandit-infested areas reminding the terrorists that there are no festivals and family reunions in the jungle.

'When will you be seeing your family again?' the leaflet asks. 'Make sure you can look forward to being with your family on festival days by giving yourselves up to the police without delay. Wait your opportunity, then slip away. Hundreds of others have done this.'

It is all very touching – and quite futile. As propaganda, it could not be wider of the mark if it had devised by a person who had never been farther East than a Whitehall office, and whose closest acquaintance with China was once having lit a Chinese cracker on Guy Fawkes night. It completely overlooks the fact that many Chinese in Malaya, law-abiding and other, have no families here, that there is still a great disparity between the sexes, and that many have left their wives in China.

While these leaflets are being dropped there arrived in Malaya Mr Carleton Greene to direct psychological warfare. He was former head of the East European service of the B.B.C. He is new to Malaya and it seems too much to expect that he will not be briefed by the very people who have blundered so badly in this department.

(*The Scotsman*, Wednesday, 4 October 1950)

intimidation were such that the villagers refused to cooperate with the authorities by identifying their Chinese Communist masters.

Two months later, escalating guerrilla activities forced the British administration to declare a state of emergency in Malaya.

This is not a definitive political or military account of the Malayan Emergency. In the twelve years of counter-insurgency operations in the British colony, regarded in the early stages as a police action against 'bandits', tens of thousands of local, British and Commonwealth armed personnel chased after a slippery enemy in an unforgiving and hostile environment. In the process, the very nature and understanding of guerrilla warfare, based on the 'armed liberation of the colonial oppressed', was redefined and overhauled.

The civilian expatriates, whether civil servant, planter, or miner, not only provided soft targets for the Communist terrorists, but also faced losing a privileged colonial life in a rapidly shrinking British Empire. Their lives in the emergency alone would fill a substantial tome. Moreover, London could not afford to forego the wealth that the peninsula provided to help repair and resuscitate the war-ravaged British economy.

For the hapless civilian population, especially the indigenous Malays, it was a nightmare. Malaya's ethnic Chinese would not assimilate with a nation in which they had spent many years – their ties with China remained undiluted.

MALAYA: 'STATE OF WAR'

Constitution Versus Communist Insurgents

"Daily Telegraph" and "The Scotsman" Correspondent

SINGAPORE, Sunday.—Gurkha troops and police fought a battle with bandits to-day, 15 miles east of Johore Bahru, after a renewal of terrorist activities in Malaya. Two of the gunmen were killed and two captured.

The highest daily toll of life since the wave of terrorism began was recorded to-day. Nine murders have been committed in the past 24 hours, and two attempts were made on Europeans.

Seven Chinese, one of them a local official of the Kuomintang Party, were killed in Johore and two in Selangor. In almost all cases the method of execution was identical. A gang of seven or eight armed Chinese dragged the victim outside, tied his hands behind him, and riddled him with bullets.

It is likely that many more attempted murders have taken place recently, especially against Europeans, but some planters and miners who escape in attacks seem reluctant to notify the police.

The authorities are making special plans for attacking jungle hide-outs. Police to-day found what is believed to be a Communist camp under construction in the jungle near Kuala Lumpur. Vegetation had been cleared and foundations laid for huts.

Siam proposes to close her border with Malay "if the situation in Malay deteriorates so as to become a threat to Siam's security." After the recent round-up of Communists in Bangkok, Siam is concerned at the danger of Communists infiltrating over the border.

GUERRILLAS MASSING IN JUNGLE

Plan to Seize Country by Revolution

FROM REUTER'S CORRESPONDENT

SINGAPORE, Sunday.—At least four to five thousand guerrillas are massing in the jungles of terror-ridden Malaya, and it will take a "minor war" to rout them out, the Singapore *Straits Times* reported to-day.

Front-page article *The Scotsman*, 28 July 1948.

By means of selective contemporary newspaper articles on the progress of the emergency, the causes, process and outcome – if indeed there was a finite one – the exclusive first-hand accounts of the Malayan experience as personally and verbally related to the author, and the author's own research, the story of the conflict emerges in the following pages.

1. DAY OF THE BUSHIDO

It is considered, therefore, in some quarters, that Malaya is in real danger of finding herself engaged in war during the next few months.

(*Aberdeen Journal*, 31 January 1941)

Capitalising on the internal ideological conflict in China between the Nationalist forces of Chiang Kai-shek and the Communist forces under Mao Zedong, the Imperial armies of Japan invaded Manchuria in September 1931. By the end of 1937, Peking, Nanking and the port city of Shanghai had fallen to the Japanese, pushing Generalissimo Chiang Kai-shek ever south.

In July 1940, Japan took French Indochina, and in a territorial trade-off with the French Vichy regime, extended its influence westwards into neighbouring Siam. Only became Thailand in 1949.

MALAYA'S DEFENCES

Let us examine the possibilities in a Japanese attack on Malaya, for Japan could never hold any part of the Indies unless she held Malaya too.

There are three usual forms of attack – land, sea, and air. An attack overland, supposing the Japanese had made their way from Indo-China into Thailand and down the Kra isthmus, can practically be ruled out. Malaya in its 600 miles of length has two railways and one main road, routes that easily can be rendered impassable.

Taking a mechanised army through the dense Malayan jungle will be about as difficult as driving a child's toy clock-work motor car through a concrete wall.

Suppose the infantry footslog along the jungle trails. Why, the primitive Sakai of the Malaysian hinterland, who have never heard of tanks or Tommy guns, using their blow pipes and poisoned darts from the forest cover, could take a sickening toll of an invader: and what if the trees hid well-armed British troops.

To make a sea attack Japanese warships must travel a long way in British or American patrolled waters. The supply routes from Japan pass uncomfortably close to the American bases in the Philippines.

Singapore is within range of Japanese bombers – until they meet our fighters. The landing of troops by air is another difficult problem, for you cannot land aeroplanes, or, for that matter, parachutists, on tree tops, and Malaya is a country of trees with very few open spaces.

And while enumerating the natural difficulties that confront a Japanese assault on Malaya we are not forgetful of the man-made difficulties – the increased strength of our forces there.

(*Western Mail*, Saturday, 2 August 1941)

The Japanese Tenth Army parades after the bloody taking of the capital of China's eastern Jiangsu province, Nanking (Nanjing), in December 1937.

British governor of the Straits Settlements, Sir Shenton Thomas, warned Britain in February 1940 that 'active war is more close to the shore of Malaya than ever before'. In spite of the vulnerability of Singapore's 'back-door ... everybody knows of the formidable defences of that focal point of the Empire's defences. Singapore is impregnable from the sea, as combined naval, aerial, and army manoeuvres before the war proved. Now the mainland of Malaya, which lies behind it, is rapidly being placed in a state of defence, and would prove a formidable obstacle to any attacker'.

For much of 1941, while apprehensively monitoring Japanese expansionism in the region, Britain continued to bolster her fighting capacity in Malaya. In August, the commander of British forces in China, Canadian-born Major General Arthur E. Grasset, confidently said, 'It is my considered opinion that unless she becomes really desperate, Japan will not be so rash as to fight Britain or the United States.'

Shortly after midnight on 8 December 1941 (local time), and just before the attack on Pearl Harbor, a Japanese attack force drawn from Lieutenant General Tomoyuki's Twenty-fifth Army, landed at Kota Bharu on Malaya's north-east coast. Basking in the morale-boosting sinking of the Royal Navy's battleship HMS *Prince of Wales* and the battlecruiser HMS *Repulse* by Japanese bombers off Kuantan in the South China Sea, the Japanese forces advanced southwards. By the end of January 1942, the whole of Malaya had fallen to the Japanese.

For the next three years, British and Commonwealth prisoners of war and the civilian Malay population suffered inhuman depravation and degradation, and a mindless pogrom of mass executions. The occupying power's unfaltering belief in the godhead emperor and a revived Bushido code of conduct legitimised atrocious actions in the name of moral purity. There was honour in death and absolute shame in weakness and failure. The act of *seppuku* – ritual suicide – was the honourable and ultimate act of atonement by the Samurai warrior who had failed the moral code of Bushido.

The uniformed disciple of the code therefore possessed an inculcated conviction that death inflicted on oneself or another to satisfy the premises of the Bushido code, was beyond question.

'AUSSIES' IN MALAYA HAVE RILED JAPAN

Thousands of cheering Australian troops have poured into Singapore, Britain's bastion in the Far East, in the last few days.

They formed the biggest force ever to arrive in Malaya in a single convoy. Their voyage and their landing was without incident.

When Japan heard the news there was evidence how unwelcome it was. 'Far from stabilising the situation in the Far East, the British action is apparently an attempt to create suspicion and distrust,' bemoaned a Japanese military spokesman in Shanghai. To cap the news of the Australians' arrival came a well-timed announcement that the Royal Air Force had been greatly strengthened in the Far East, too.

I watched the Australian troops arrive at Singapore to the strains of 'Roll Out the Barrel', and the heartfelt cheers of thousands of spectators on the quaysides (writes the B.U.P. correspondent there).

As the Australians disembarked, the watchers on land could see how complete a unit it was. Not only was there infantry, artillery and signallers, but nursing units and all ancillary services, supply depots, an Australian general hospital, artillery regiments equipped with the most modern howitzers and field guns (manufactured in Australia), anti-tank units, many fully mechanised infantry battalions, and an Australian Army Service Corps unit with its own transport.

The men had been trained as storm troops and it can be safely said that if they were called upon to defend this outpost of Australia they would fight as their fathers did in Gallipoli, France and Palestine, and as their brothers had recently done in Libya.

(*Daily Record*, Thursday, 20 February 1941)

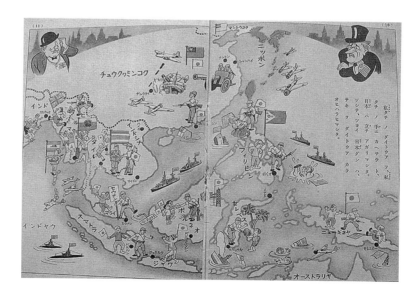

Japanese Asian propaganda poster 1943.

The anti-Japanese ethnic Chinese in Malaya, seen as a direct threat to the will of the emperor, had to be eliminated. The *Sook Ching* (purge through cleansing) genocide, centred in Singapore on the tip of the Malay Peninsula, spilled north. Military police of the Japanese occupation army – *kempeitai* – zealously massacred an estimated 100,000 ethnic Chinese.

The British Special Operations Executive formed Force 136, headquartered in Ceylon and responsible for training and arming anti-Japanese resistance movements in the Southeast Asia theatre. Early in the Japanese invasion, Captain Freddie Chapman, an experienced mountaineer and adventurer, joined the Special Training School 101 (STS 101), and for eighteen months he had to endure hardship, hunger and disease, living with Communist Chinese guerrillas in the Malayan jungles, eluding the Japanese. Eventually, in 1945, the indomitable Chapman escaped from Malaya on board the submarine HMS *Statesman*.

It was only then that Chapman's jungle sojourn could be shared with the British public. On 20 September 1945, the British *Daily Mirror* carried a report by journalist George McCarthy:

> From the time Malaya fell into the hands of the Japanese in December 1941, a party of British-led guerrillas carried on the war from their secret fortresses deep in the heart of the jungle.
>
> There, in one of the loneliest places on earth they made friends with the aboriginal natives – the Sakai – a people so shy that they never venture into towns or villages.
>
> It was among these people who still hunt with blowpipe and bow and arrow that Lieutenant Colonel Freddie Chapman, peacetime explorer and leader of the party, hid for months with the little army of Chinese guerrillas he had trained.

The Malayan People's Anti-Japanese Army MPAJA at a disbanding ceremony in December 1945. (Source *The War Illustrated*)

The tribesmen had emerged from centuries of obscurity to help a hunted army. Before they had to run, Chapman and his band, in a series of brilliant raids, had killed between 500 and 1,000 Japs, cut railways and destroyed transport behind the enemy lines.

With the Sakai, Chapman and his men learned jungle tricks and taught the Sakai some in return.

In 1943, Captain R.N. Broome, Malaya Civil Service, and Captain J.L.H. Davis, Malaya Police, sneaked into Malaya and joined Chapman.

Once they escaped capture by a hair's breadth. A Chinese merchant who had befriended them was caught and tortured; their jungle camp was attacked, and their code, maps, money and medicine lost.

But they carried on. Then, early in 1945, it became necessary for British officers to leave Malaya to report. Chapman and Broome, in darkness swam out to a grounded British submarine. They made their getaway to build a new army.

And in India and Ceylon a new force was raised, which in June this year began to drop into Malaya. When the Japs surrendered, 300 men had landed, and 2,500 Chinese and Malayan guerrillas had been armed and trained.

Chapman's Malayan legacy was a well-honed and jungle-seasoned core of Communist guerrillas who, shortly after the surrender of Japanese forces in the region, were to turn their arms and skills against the British with the objective of driving them out of Malaya.

Royal Marines of the East Indies Fleet parade on the Penang quayside at the raising of the Union Jack following the Japanese surrender in this part of the peninsula. (Source *The War Illustrated*)

AUSTRALIA DEMANDS LESSON FOR JAPS

A public demand throughout Australia that Japan must be taught 'a lesson she will never forget' has followed the publication of the Webb report on Japanese atrocities. The report has stirred up the most bitter anti-Japanese feeling in the Commonwealth, the *Sydney Sun* declares.

'With comparatively weak forces in occupation of Japan the safety of captives must be the first consideration,' says the paper. 'Nevertheless the Japanese must learn the hard way that calamity has befallen them.'

When an Australian party flew to Sandakan, once a large Japanese prisoner-of-war centre in North Borneo, the Japanese reported that no prisoners remained alive in the camp, an Australian Army statement said today. Official Japanese figures obtained elsewhere stated that at one stage 3,726 prisoners, including 1,900 Australians, were held at Sandakan.

Allied troops were today spreading through the Japanese home islands as the demobilisation and disarming of Japanese forces went on smoothly, General MacArthur's headquarters announced.

Hideki Tojo, the prime minister who led Japan into the war, was reported ten days ago to be alive and preparing his defence against war crime charges, according to a Tokio [sic] report.

Field Marshal Terauchi, Supreme Jap Commander, Southern Region, has had a stroke and is seriously ill at Saigon, said New Delhi radio today. According to a British officer who saw him at Saigon, Terauchi, who is over 70, is unlikely to attend the surrender ceremony at Singapore on Wednesday, the report added.

Commenting on the series of 'evasions and equivocations' over the surrender of Count Terauchi the Service newspaper 'Seac' wrote:

'Japanese impudence has been manifest from the start of this surrender and it does not decrease as the days pass. It will get worse yet if it is not stopped. There is more than loutishness in this. There is political design. These people are saving their face by spitting on ours.'

Five-hundred Japanese officers are reported to have committed *hara kiri* at the end of a farewell cocktail party in Singapore after the news of the Japanese surrender, said Singapore radio today.

(*Dundee Evening Telegraph*, Monday, 10 September 1945)

2. CHAIRMAN MAO'S PROTÉGÉS

The Balkans have always been, and still are, the powder keg of world unrest. But another area has arisen from which the fires of conflict will spring – Southeast Asia and the former Far East battleground.

Today the area is in the melting pot, and in no fewer than six countries the fires of independence and revolution are spreading, threatening to consume their economic, social and personal structure and throwing millions, who have already suffered long years of war, into another boiling tumult of suffering, looting, famine, pestilence and unrest.

(N.W. Cutler, *Lincolnshire Echo* Far East observer, 13 December 1945)

The ink on Japan's instruments of unconditional surrender barely dry, war-suppressed nationalist fervour started to resurface across Southeast Asia.

In Java, Indonesian activists, kitted out with recently acquired Japanese equipment, started making it known in unequivocal terms that they had no desire to see their Dutch masters return to their homelands.

Supreme Allied commander, Lord Louis Mountbatten, was given carte blanche to stamp out the insurrection, even full-scale military operations to restore law and order. On 3 September 1945, General Philip Christison, deputising for Mountbatten, received the surrender of the Japanese Seventh Area Army and South Sea Fleet at Singapore. Two months later, Christison's troops engaged Indonesian liberation forces in a full-scale battle.

In 1945, Soviet forces invaded Manchuria, resulting in the almost immediate capitulation of the occupying Japanese forces. To complicate the scenario further, the People's Liberation Army of China had launched its civil war operations from safe bases in Manchuria, and after that, to provide North Korea with military muscle against United Nations forces.

Strained Soviet–American relations were therefore not restricted to the Berlin and German impasse. Moscow refused to withdraw her troops from Manchuria, retaining hundreds of tanks and artillery pieces along the Manchuria-China demarcation line. Repeated American requests to the Russians for coal from North Korea to meet the needs of US troops in South Korea were refused. Japanese troops under Russian 'care' were indoctrinated with Communism before repatriation to Japan.

In China itself, the Nationalist government of Chiang Kai-shek and the Communist Chinese usurpers continued with their five-year-old fight.

With the Berlin crisis threatening to escalate into yet another global conflict, but this time between the United States and the Soviet Union, US Secretary of State James F. Byrnes declared that America's post-war international foreign policy was designed to rehabilitate war-ravaged economies, not just in Western Europe and Britain under the Marshall Plan, but also in Nationalist China. 'We favour a strong China, united and democratic,' he said.

Russia's expansionist designs on the region, particularly in northern China, were very apparent to Washington. Rumours, however, were also rife of a liaison between Yennen, the Communist headquarters in China, and the Kremlin.

Chiang Kai-shek, leader of the Republic of China between 1928 and 1975. (Source *The War Illustrated*)

Britain chose to distance herself from events in the Far East, electing instead to monitor a growing wave of pressure from Malaya and Burma for independence. In Malaya, the situation was exacerbated by a marked lack of national cohesion among the three main ethnic groups: Chinese, Malaya and Indian. The worrying reality for London was the fact that the Chinese outnumbered the indigenous Malays, while the Indians were in the minority.

Identifying the need for an evolutionary process, Britain opted for a dominion-style status for the rubber- and tin-rich Malayan Peninsula.

The Malayan Communist Party (MCP) has its origins in April 1930 when the South Seas Communist Party folded, to be replaced by national Communist parties in Indochina, Malaya and Siam.

FATHER CHRISTMAS PLANES WILL SUPPLY SEAC

British soldiers in Java, Sumatra, and other remote parts of the South East Asia Command, will get their Christmas pudding after all. Even the handful of men clearing up on Christmas Island will get an English Christmas dinner.

The famous 'Flying Horse' Squadron of Transport Command is providing a fleet of 'Father Christmas' aeroplanes which will fly Christmas supplies to Java and Sumatra, including the NAAFI turkeys. Some will go up to Sourabaya, scene of Java's worst fighting, so men of the West Yorkshire Regiment are sure of their Christmas dinner.

Other supplies will go to Batavia, where elaborate Christmas plans are now being laid on for men of the 1st Seaforth Highlanders, the 7th Paratroop Brigade (men of Arnhem), RAF men, and men of all British units.

Singapore is becoming chockful of Christmas puddings flown in daily or arriving by ship. Sentries mount guard over them for fear of 'black market' looters.

Every man in the Indies will get 10 bottles of beer for Christmas week and 75 cigarettes. But he will have to pay for them.

One steamer is heading from Calcutta with a cargo of pork, ham and poultry for Malaya, Sumatra, Java and Borneo. The cargo will be flown into Indonesia from Singapore.

The Seaforths in Batavia are to throw an outsize in Christmas parties for thousands of Dutch, Chinese and Eurasian evacuee children in Java, and if I know my Seaforths, a lot of Christmas fare meant for them will find its way to the mouths of these children who have so recently known three years of starvation diet in Japanese prison camps.

(*Western Mail*, Monday, 17 December 1945)

In spite of early setbacks, such as being proscribed by Britain, by the mid-1930s the MCP had become increasingly active in fomenting civil unrest through the establishment of workers' committees at selected workplaces in the country. The colonial authorities, however, dealt quickly and unforgivingly with these Communist cells. Striking ethnic Chinese arrested by the police and troops were immediately deported to China, where they were labelled Communists and summarily executed by the Nationalist government of Chiang Kai-shek.

The party structure was typical of the Communist model, with a central executive committee and politburo at the apex. Below this national coordinating and decision-making body, were conceptually similar state and district committees, right down to the grassroots cell at the village or workplace level.

After an ignominious fall from grace, in March 1947 MCP secretary general Lai Teck made a hasty exit into neighbouring Siam, allegedly after pilfering the party coffers. The staunch Communist Chin Peng filled the MCP leadership void.

Born in Malaya's Perak State, the 26-year-old ethnic Chinese was a veteran of clandestine resistance guerrilla activities against the Japanese invaders. Operating in conjunction with British SOE operatives, Chin Peng was awarded the OBE for his services to the Crown.

In May 1948, the MCP politburo met at a secret, remote venue in the dense jungles of Pahang State. In a large camp hidden in the sparsely populated rainforest between the towns

Chin Peng, leader of The Malayan Communist Party. (Source not found)

of Raub and Bentong, north-east of the capital Kuala Lumpur, fifty regional Communist leaders spent little time in deliberation to unanimously agree to the use of force to wrench Malaya away from the British.

In their ranks were the MCP's key propagandist, the twenty-four-year-old ethnic Chinese Osman China, Ah ' Shorty' Kuk, commander of the Jahore State Communists, and head of the armed forces, Lau Yew – names that would become synonymous with the impending conflict.

The 5,000-strong Malayan Races Liberation Army (MRLA) was formed to spearhead the armed insurrection. British-trained by the SOE's Force 136 during the Japanese occupation, these veterans of jungle warfare drew their arms and materiel from scattered caches of an array of weaponry parachuted into the jungle by British forces during the anti-Japanese guerrilla campaign. Numerous well-concealed Force 136 base camps, situated strategically across the peninsula, would be refurbished to barrack the equivalent of eight regiments of the MRLA.

The Communist terrorists or CTs as they would commonly be called, employed simple tactics in the model of Mao Zedong's rural revolution – swift, random, hit-and-run attacks that were brutal in the extreme. Murder and terror would be the norm. The CTs' biggest advantage in the jungle battleground was the element of surprise, where ambush-encompassed killing zones could be meticulously laid out for optimum results.

Integral to the success of the revolution was the presence of 'sleepers' loyal to the cause – schoolteachers, civil servants, waiters, plantation workers, medical workers in the mainstream

Lee Hong Kwong, charismatic Communist terrorist (CT) leader. (Courtesy Rhodesian African Rifles Regimental Association (UK))

of Malayan life who would be the civilian eyes and ears of the armed force. Called the Min Yuen – mass movement – these agents would also be the prime source of information, food and money. To the British, they were sympathisers.

In two separate incidents, early on 16 June 1948, the press broke the news that three British planters in Malaya had been murdered by 'Chinese terrorists'. The callous executions of Messrs Walker, Allison and Christian were interpreted as the commencement of 'the second phase of the "Red Plan" to conquer Malaya'.

A special correspondent with *The Press and Journal*, reported in the 17 June 1948 edition, that the 'plan' had been drawn up by the leaders of anti-Japanese guerrilla forces who had 'declared their own war on British Malaya a few weeks after the Japanese surrender'.

I saw a copy of this plan six months ago, taken from the body of a slain gunman. It laid down that, parallel with an open attempt to capture the trade unions, a secret organisation whose members were not known to the legal Communist Party here, would hold itself in readiness for terrorist activities: 'We must attack British imperialists first, even combining with National Capitalists (meaning Chinese) until we have ousted the British,' the plan said.

The gang which killed the Perak planters this morning told native workers, 'We are killing only Europeans.'

Less than a fortnight later, an estimated group of forty heavily armed CTs attacked and captured the remote village of Jerantut in central Pahang, seventy-five miles north-east of Kuala Lumpur. After cutting the telephone wires, the terrorists opened fire on the flimsy police station. The doomed occupants lasted until their ammunition ran out. Their assailants then set the building on fire. A hapless villager caught while running between two huts, was caught, tied to a pole, and blown to pieces with a shotgun fired at close range. The executed man's wife and two daughters were then bound and thrown into a hut which was then put to the torch.

The ordinary citizen of Malaya had been ruthlessly introduced to the abject trademark terror of a Communist-inspired revolution. As intended, the bloody message spread quickly – comply or face a lingering, horrific death. Days later, a Malay policeman endured excruciating pain inflicted at the hands of three CTs. As he futilely fought for his life in the village of Layang Layang in Jahore State, shock-numbed villagers gazed at the sickening act being played out in front of them. Theirs would be the same macabre fate should they dare speak of the identity of these harbingers of terror and death.

TROOPS MASS AS FRENCH RIOTS SPREAD

Rioting strikers in France's 'rubber capital' of Clermont-Ferrand tonight massed behind street barricades in preparation for a second night of pitched battle with 4,000 armed mobile guards and police besieging the town.

New tension sprang up as groups of Communist-led toughs began roaming the streets at nightfall armed with blackjacks and iron bars.

Five-hundred Republican security guards were flown to Clermont-Ferrand tonight from Lyons. More police reinforcements have also been moved in to back up steel-helmeted Republican guards patrolling the main city avenues with armoured cars.

Tanks are standing by and infantry troops are being held on rapid-move orders at barracks round the town.

A growing number of workers converging on the troubled area include a strong contingent of foreigners, it was officially announced last night. Strikes in protest against the clashes at Clermont-Ferrand spread to Marseilles, where all municipal workers were called to observe a four-hour 'sympathy strike' this morning.

(*Aberdeen Journal*, Thursday, 17 June 1948)

REWARDS
for information

Substantial **REWARDS** will be paid to all who co-operate with the authorities in providing information about Intimidators and Gangsters.

The source of all information given to the Police is kept Secret.

Up to **$2,000** have been paid to a person who has given useful Information.

Communicate with the Police by every means possible.

Useful Information
EARNS
CASH

EMERGENCY REGULATIONS

are

NOW IN FORCE

HOW DO THEY AFFECT

YOU?

Malayan government reward pamphlet.

3. RUBBER AND TIN EMPIRES

For that purpose [establishing a Communist republic in Malaya], the Communist terrorists launched attacks on the rubber estates and tin mines in the Malay States. These attacks had caused the destruction to the rubber estates and tin mines. They destroyed the mining engines, burnt down smoke houses, factories, hostels or *kongsi* houses and offices; slashed rubber trees and others. In addition, the labourers, miners and planters who wouldn't cooperate with them were brutally murdered. The aim was to terrorize and instil fear into the mind that brought a disruptive influence on their work and their daily lives. This was what the Communist terrorists wanted, to cause unemployment among the labourers.

(Dr Ho Hui Ling, History Department, University of Malaya)

Since early in the sixteenth century, the Portuguese, Dutch and English manifested their respective trading interests in the lands of Southeast Asia, in their quest to satisfy a burgeoning demand for pepper, spices and other exotic products, fuelled by the significant growth in national economies.

Competing with the Dutch East Indies Company's dominance in the region, the English East India Company established revictualling posts at Penang, Singapore and Melaka in support of increased trade with China. The flourishing trade attracted Chinese migrants keen on establishing businesses, as well as wage-labour in an expanding production of gold and tin for export. At the time, the indigenous races on the peninsula were sustaining a subsistence living based on the commercial production of rice and tin.

By the mid-1800s, the Industrial Revolution was catapulting Western economies into factory-based mass production. The demand for both raw materials and foodstuffs for better-off populations grew exponentially. Regions such as Southeast Asia, already established as trade staging posts, offered virgin land with the potential to meet the West's increased craving for consumables such as coffee, sugar and pepper.

As British economic interests in the Malayan Peninsula solidified, geological surveys revealed significant tin deposits in the states of Perak and Selangor. Dwindling output from exhausted Cornwall tin mines, combined with a major surge in canned-food production, made the large-scale exploitation of tin deposits in Malaya viable. By the end of the nineteenth century, at 52,000 tons, Malayan tin accounted for more than half the world's total output. The mines attracted large numbers of Chinese migrant wage-labour.

Edward VII's succession to the British throne saw a significant wane in export-crop production on the peninsula, as unsustainable price fluctuations, and pests and diseases undermined viability.

As early as the 1870s, the British government had conducted trials to see if rubber trees sourced from Brazil could be grown in the tropical regions of some of her colonies, such as Singapore and Ceylon. The rubber tree – *Hevea brasiliensis* – demanded long-term investment as it needed five years of nurturing before coming into production. The success of the experimental project surpassed all expectations, resulting in a flood of English and Chinese investors establishing rubber plantations in swathes of cleared jungle.

Tapping latex from a rubber tree on an estate in Malaya. (Courtesy John Anderson)

By 1921, 1.3 million acres of Malaysia was under rubber, mainly in the Malayan Peninsula. Of this acreage, expatriate Europeans owned 75 per cent of the large estate plantations. The British drew their migrant labour from the Indian sub-continent, while the Chinese enterprises relied on the so-called 'coolie trade' from the southern parts of China.

The much-improved living standards for these migrants persuaded many to settle in Malaya permanently. A multi-ethnic society evolved, and in some regions, indigenous Malayans found themselves in the minority.

Chinese entrepreneurial aspirations translated into this ethnic group dominating large commercial centres in Penang, Kuching and Singapore, as well as the small trader in towns and villages. Together with substantial ownership of mines and agricultural property, wealth and therefore economic power gravitated towards the ethnic Chinese.

During the Japanese occupation of the Second World War, the peninsula's vibrant economy collapsed. Only limited primary output was permitted, and then only for Japanese industry. Rubber plantations and tin mines were abandoned, and Chinese enterprises expropriated on

CIVILISING MALAYA

There is a most gratifying consensus of opinion on the part of those who know anything about the subject in favour of annexing the southern extremity of the Malay Peninsula, which has acquired so melancholy a notoriety by the murder of Mr Birch [British administrator]. One who knows the Peninsula well declares that Mr Birch would have gladly met his death if he could have foreseen that, by the sacrifice of his life, Malaya would be saved, for its annexation by Great Britain would be nothing short of its temporal salvation.

The ridiculous hubbub made over the rising in Perak [fourth largest state in Malaya] – a hubbub due almost entirely to an ignorance of the facts which we had before our readers immediately the news of Mr Birch's fate reached us by telegram – is not entirely to be lamented, if it leads – as it appears likely to lead – in the extension of our sovereignty over the whole of the disturbed districts.

A great deal of unnecessary expense has, however, been incurred in the way of sending troops to suppress a mere local outbreak. This excessive reliance upon Imperial aid is natural but pernicious. If Sir W. Jervois [governor of the Straits Settlements] had been left to his own resources, he would have been able to suppress the outbreak of the Malay Rajahs in Perak by the proffered aid of the Chinese ... so long as we have the Chinese on our side we have nothing to fear.

Whatever the Malays think of annexation, the Chinese have declared before this that there is not a Chinaman in Perak who would not go down on his knees and bless God when the British flag was hoisted in the capital.

(Northern Echo, Monday, 22 November 1875)

behalf of the emperor. Under the cloak of least-favoured ethnic group, the Chinese bore the brunt of the brutal governance of the Japanese military.

With the defeat of Japan in 1945, Britain wasted no time in resuscitating the colony's export economy to pre-war levels. Gula-Kalumpong Rubber Estates alone had announced that '990 acres of rubber, out of 9,050 acres, have been destroyed by the Japanese, also a large proportion of plant and buildings'. Reconstruction of the infrastructure and rehabilitation of tin and rubber production allowed the thousand white planters – virtually all British – to return to their dormant properties. Here, the expatriates restored their livelihood and colonial lifestyle. Eight hundred European – a euphemism for non-Asian – miners, including American nationals, also returned to their diggings, around which small communities had grown.

In January 1946, a parliamentary white paper was issued laying out proposals to regroup the Straits Settlements – Singapore, Malacca, Dinding and Penang – and the Malay states to form the Colony of Singapore and the Malayan Union. Mr Malcolm MacDonald was appointed commissioner-general designate for Southeast Asia. Upon the second reading of the bill, the Under-Secretary for Colonies, Mr Creech Jones, pointed out that the government's objective was to secure a stable, single union embodying common citizenship. He stressed timing was

A Malayan rubber plantation manager's bungalow. (Courtesy John Anderson)

critical, as a return to 'the old system, with its divided loyalties and backwardness' would be totally undesirable.

Creech implored the diverse peoples of the peninsula to cooperate: 'It is not annexation, but fulfilment – not Imperialism, but an effort to carry out faithfully our economic liabilities.'

On 1 April, Sir Edward Gent was installed as governor of the newly formed Malay Union. Westminster formalisation of the national entity, however, was immediately met with disfavour in the capital, Kuala Lumpur.

Two days after Gent assumed office, demonstrators gathered outside the city hotel where the traditional Malay rulers were staying after they had boycotted the governor's installation ceremony. The crowd expressed their loyalty with chants of 'long live the sultans' and 'long live the Malays'. The Malay members of the Advisory Council boycotted the first meeting of the body called by the governor.

In May, Malcolm MacDonald took up his position as Governor General of the Malayan Union and Singapore.

In a landmark international rubber-marketing arrangement in June 1946, Britain, the Netherlands, France and the United States signed an agreement that would allow America to buy rubber directly from Malaya, rather than via Britain. Malayan rubber experts, however, expressed disappointment with the Anglo-American agreement that fixed the price of rubber at 1s 2d a pound. They believed that the Malayan industry needed total reorganisation to remain competitive with synthetic products entering the market. Mr R.P. Hardwick, a thirty-five-year veteran of the Malayan rubber industry, urged government to subsidise the complete replanting of plantations with high-yielding trees that would boost production by up to 400 per cent.

Brigadier John 'Digger' Essex-Clark came into regular contact with planters and miners in his tour of duty during the emergency. He speaks of their lives under CT threat:

> Plantation and tin mine owners often knew more about the areas of their responsibilities than did the Malay Police and Special Branch because they spoke regularly with their workers and knew their fears and any Min Yuen activity.
>
> At times, to avoid friction with the CT and resulting loss of workers, their own and their families' lives, and economic disadvantage (commercial failure) the owners of plantations and tin mines would side with and even support the CT, but those understandably scared owners did not last long as they were spirited away back to the UK or elsewhere by the British internal security system of which I know nothing except that the owners disappeared. If it was a terrorist rather than a system removal, it was supported by rather gruesome detail left by the CT. So many of those owners lived on a knife edge and most left their families safely ensconced in Singapore or the 'White area'd' Penang. Nevertheless, many managers

A Malayan 'planter' armed with a 9mm Sten gun for self-protection. (Courtesy John Anderson)

or owners of rubber or palm oil estates or tin mines in Malaya lived very precariously. One could get much info out of them if you befriended and protected them by intensive patrolling of their plantations and mines. Welcome them into your company's officers' mess and they reciprocated using their often lavish homes. One spent a few evenings showing me and explaining horse brasses, amongst interesting but subtle intelligence about the CT and Min Yuen operating in his area. As a non sequitur: one of his horse brasses had cost him thousands of pounds; so he was reasonably well off. I think that they were well-paid for the risks they took. Many 'lived native' and had delightful Malay or Chinese wives.

John Anderson, a civilian from Britain who had served in the Royal Navy during the Second World War, arrived in Malaya in April 1950, to take up a position as an assistant on a rubber plantation twelve miles west of Kuala Lumpur, on the main road to Port Swettenham. In an exclusive interview with the author in November 2016, John spoke of his stay in the country, working in the rubber industry. At the time, as a 21-year-old bachelor, John recalls, with great humour, his eye-opening welcome to the colony:

I had two scares within the first forty-eight hours. As I left the ship in Penang, there was a shot, and somebody, somewhere, was shot just within a couple of hundred yards of me. I don't know who it was.

A PLANTER IN MALAYA

'The Confessions of a Planter in Malaya', by Leopold Ainsworth, is published at price 10s 6d by Messrs H.F. & G. Witherby, London. It is an intimate, well-written book about a country in which there are great British interests.

From the author's observations during many years of travel, Malaya is the only country in which poverty does not bring hardship and discomfort upon those who are actually poor from the money point of view.

Occasionally Malaya comes under a deluge, and on one occasion the author notes, the rain gauge showed that over ten inches of rain had fallen in five hours. There is a curious story about two frog visitors to a bungalow, and among other things they puffed away at a cigarette, evidently, enjoying it.

To live the life of a planter, Mr Ainsworth says, one must love one's job to the exclusion of everything else. The Malay's manner he describes as frank, open, and cheerful. He is one of nature's gentlemen in the best sense of the word. The author mentions that he was, after very hard and exhausting work, massaged by Malays, who are adepts at this form of treatment, and have an amazing knowledge of anatomy. It has always amazed Mr Ainsworth that massage is not more generally used in Western countries, for it is his experience that one can be revived from a state of exhaustion to one of comparative freshness in a very short space of time, and that all manner of aches, pains, and strains can be rapidly cured by it.

(*Edinburgh Evening News*, Friday, 20 October 1933)

Then, I got on the train in the morning, and when I arrived in Kuala Lumpur I was met by a chap, another planter – Chris Booker – and he says, 'Oh, was this train held up today?' I said, 'No, why?' to which Booker nonchalantly comments, 'Oh, it's the first time it got through in three weeks!'

I spent that night with Booker, not in my own bungalow. In the morning, he got up and went off, after telling me to stay there, have a rest, and get over the journey and everything, and he'd be back by eight. Just before eight, I got a telephone call, and I answered the phone wondering what language it was going to be. It was the clerk in the office who said, 'We have just heard that Mr Booker has been shot in the field.' He wanted me to come to the office, so I signalled one of the special constables – we each had special constables living with us; seven for a bachelor – and left with him for the office. Fortunately, just as I got there, Booker drove up from the other way.

The police had come, and what I thought was a terrible thing at that time, they arrived in soft-skin vehicles. There had been many arguments about this at the top levels of government, and eventually the police received armoured vehicles.

What had actually happened, was that the terrorists had been on the estate and the man I had been sent to replace had been killed. His name was Jimmy Chalmers. When I arrived at

John Anderson in his office on the plantation where he was employed, a .45 Colt 1911 pistol at the ready on his desk. (Courtesy John Anderson)

Plantation management were required to take Malayan police special constables with them wherever they went. (Courtesy John Anderson)

the office, Booker informed me that he had been seen by a congenitally deaf rubber-tapper, who also observed an unknown number of Communist terrorists following him. The tapper then ran to the office to report what he had seen and that Booker had been shot. He was, of course, wrong. The terrorists were never found.

Chalmers had in fact been out on his motorbike, and after his murder, motorbikes were banned on the estates.

[The 25-year-old James Chalmers was murdered by CTs on 3 October 1950. Assistant estate manager at Kinrara Estate, Chalmers had been out walking his bull terrier when he was shot at point-blank range from a clump of banana trees. The first shot wounded him, and after the gang killed the dog, they killed him. Chalmers, who came from Banffshire in Scotland, had been in Malaya for two and a half years. During the Second World War, he served with the RAF as a flight engineer.]

Anderson had been sent by his employer, Harrison and Crossfield of London, to recruit planters as a result of staff losses since troubles began in 1948. This hugely successful international tea-trader had, in 1905, diversified some of its Malayan interests into the production of rubber.

At this stage of the emergency, the introduction of armoured vehicles for civilians was still in its early stages. Anderson's personal transport was a new, open-top Morris Minor, and it was only when he was posted north to an estate near the Thai border, as assistant estate manager,

Above: John Anderson's open-top Morris, protected by a special constable carrying a 9mm Sten gun. (Courtesy John Anderson)

Left: An armed John Anderson in front of a plantation of young rubber trees. (Courtesy John Anderson)

that he was given an armoured Land Rover for his job. After the Morris Minor, Anderson purchased his much-loved MG sports car:

> I had a bullet hole through the petrol tank one night, about nine miles off the main road towards the estate. This was in Kedah [state] near the Thai border. I was going home in the evening and somebody shot at me from the jungle through which I passed. But it wasn't a proper ambush and not very accurate. We never found out anything about it, although the assistant on the next-door estate had been shot in the leg.

Anderson's first weapon for protection was a 'useless thing called a Colt automatic, which would have been the .45-calibre American M1911 pistol. At the time, civilians used personal weapons, but in due course, Anderson was issued with a .30-calibre American army M1 carbine, which he described as 'an excellent weapon, wonderful for shooting pigs ... I didn't have to shoot anybody with it, but I shot lots of pigs'. Eventually, Anderson had no fewer than seven firearms in his bungalow.

The CT penchant for ambushes meant that particular thought and care was demanded when travelling. Anderson explains:

> We never told anybody where we were going on the estate. Nearly all the planters who were killed died in ambushes. There were a hundred of them, which was 10 per cent of the planters at the time.

A civilian convoy forms up, waiting for an armed escort before departure. (Courtesy John Anderson)

We were banned from certain areas, before the so-called black areas were introduced. We didn't go into the rubber after three o'clock in certain places. There was a daily curfew between the hours of 7.00 pm to 6.00 am. In fact, I was almost shot by the Rhodesian Rifles [Rhodesian African Rifles] because I was in the wrong place at the wrong time.

We could only do our shopping on certain days. Once done, we had to get our shopping bills signed, and then we had to join a military convoy as we were carrying food.

Plantation estate managerial employees, key to the ongoing production of rubber to feed substantial post-war demand, were especially vulnerable to the CT modus operandi. As Anderson explains, much was therefore done by the estate owners and the British administration to protect these assets:

Bachelors had seven special constables living with them in their bungalow. I had a raised bungalow, and they used to live underneath. They were exclusively Malays. There may have been one or two Chinese or Indians, but I never met them. This fits in with the civil service all being in the hands of the Malays.

I had one fellow, a wonderful chap – Abii Rouser. He was a Batar [from Sarawak, Borneo], and he polished his .303 rifle, and he polished all the rounds. He was a jolly good bodyguard.

PRE-WAR LIFE IN MALAYA CONDEMNED

Biting criticism of the pre-war life of Europeans in Malaya is contained in a book on the campaign in that country, written by Gilbert Mant, formerly Reuter's special correspondent with the British Forces in Malaya.

The book, 'Grim Glory', has a foreword by Major-General Gordon Bennett, who commanded the Australian Forces and escaped after the fall of Singapore.

Europeans in Malaya, writes Mant, suffered from acute class consciousness and moral flabbiness. They led a 'preposterously spoilt artificial existence', with life just a round of leisured boredom resulting in an atmosphere of 'tidapathy' – coined from the Malayan 'tidapa', meaning 'it does not matter'.

Although there were many fine examples of courage and self-sacrifice during the fighting among men and women alike, there was an underlying feeling of helplessness and complete inability to understand the causes of the catastrophe.

The evacuation of Penang, Mant describes as the 'sorriest chapter of the whole Malayan campaign.'

The author sums up the campaign in the following words:

'The battle of Malaya was lost before it started. It was lost in the myth of Singapore's impregnability. It was lost by the gross under-estimation of Japan's strength and military cleverness. It was lost in the belief that it was impossible to use tanks in Malaya.'

Australia, he adds, cannot escape her share of the blame.

(*Coventry Evening Telegraph*, Thursday, 16 July 1942)

In spite of the constant terrorist threat, club functions for British expatriates and wealthy Malays were not forsaken. (Courtesy John Anderson)

Walking through the rubber one day, we couldn't find any tappers. They had all been rounded up and were being lectured by the Communists on the benefits of Communism, or whatever they lectured them on. Rouser ran forward – you get $2,000 for capturing a live terrorist – firing these polished rounds from the hip, and of course they all fled. They could have shot him down, but they were off. There were about five of them, and we believed they had walked along the power line from Kuala Lumpur. By the time the police were informed and got there, they were gone.

The constables escorted us everywhere – not all seven, you usually took one or occasionally two if we were going to a hotspot. We used to have to take them even into Kuala Lumpur when I lived near there, and deposit them with the weapons – their weapons and my weapons – at the police station and collect them on the way back.

I used to have to pay – well I quite gladly paid – several of the SCs [special constables] enough on such occasions to go to the pictures, while I went to see my friends. We had what were called planters' clubs, but only because they had been started long ago by planters – anyone could join.

The drive home was sometimes a little bit hairy. Nearly everybody drank White Label whisky [Dewar's blended Scotch whisky popular on the American market]. Not G&T [gin and tonic]. Ladies and some of the planters may have had G&Ts lunchtime, but of an evening the answer was whisky and water – never with ice.

In spite of the ever-present terrorist threat and risk of being ambushed, the planter community tried as much as possible to lead normal lives. Managers had been attested as 'honorary inspectors' in the police force. Travel was not permitted without at least one special constable,

A special constable with his issue .303 SMLE rifle. (Courtesy John Anderson)

and strict food-movement regulations was often bothersome. Especially for the young bachelors, such as John Anderson, recreation was a prerequisite to living in British Malaya. For many of the estate employees, however, this was not the case. Anderson gives his views:

I didn't feel a great difference. I mean, I would go to the club – the planters' club – every Thursday night for a film, and meet a few other planters and drink whisky.

But the general populace, I think they had depression. I know on one estate I lived there were times when a gang of Communists used to come in and sleep on the estate – not because the labourers were pro-Communist, but they were terrorised.

[Did they ever kill any of the labourers?] Oh yes, labourers were shot. They would usually be shot for cooperating with the authorities. They were out in the fields – in the rubber – exposed, by themselves, unarmed. I mean, easy pickings. They just had to be careful.

Right: A .303-armed special constable on guard duty at a planter's bungalow. (Courtesy John Anderson)

Below: Malayan police force special constables on rubber plantation deployment. (Courtesy John Anderson)

For post-war Western economies, the strategic security of Southeast Asia was an imperative. For the United Kingdom, political tenureship of her colonies in the region was of fundamental importance not only for economic and social reconstruction, but also for industrial expansion.

Addressing the House of Commons in July 1946 during a debate on the Colonial Development and Welfare Act, Colonial Secretary George Hall declared that the 'idea of one people dominating another was repugnant to the Government. It was not domination that they sought. But neither was it their intention to abandon peoples who had come to depend on us for their security and wellbeing'. He advocated a move to self-government in the colonies 'as fast as they showed themselves capable of going'.

Hall added that his office was studying what further measures could be taken to improve the marketing of colonial produce and to protect colonial producers from the harmful effects of world-market fluctuations. West Bristol Conservative Member of Parliament Colonel Stanley contended that government's colonial focus over the next few years 'should not be on the political but on the social and economic side. We had a much bigger leeway to catch up there than in the machinery of government.'

Fellow backbenchers on both sides of the House, however, warned of political uncertainty in Malaya. The nine Sultans still claimed that they signed the union agreement under duress. MPs Captain L.D. Gammans and Lieutenant Colonel D.R. Rees-Williams spoke of their experiences in a recent visit to Malaya, in which Gammans recalled:

'THE TIGER OF MALAYA' HANGED

General [Tomoyuki] Yamashita, 'the Tiger of Malaya' and conqueror of Singapore, was today hanged as a war criminal.

Yamashita, who was sentenced to death by a US military tribunal for permitting atrocities when he was Japanese C-in-C in the Philippines, met his death on a scaffold erected at a place 35 miles outside Manila. Two other Japanese were executed at the same time.

The general's last words were, 'I will pray for the Emperor's long life and his prosperity for ever'. As he stepped up to the scaffold accompanied by a priest and an interpreter, he appeared calm and stoical, according to the US army announcement of the execution.

Yamashita was responsible for the deaths of more than 25,000 men, women and children, and for the mass executions of US prisoners.

An hour after Yamashita was hanged, Lieutenant Colonel Seiichi Ohta, head of the dreaded secret police in Manila and the most hated man in Manila, and Akuma Higashiji, a civilian interpreter, followed him to the gallows.

Higashiji, who during his trial laughed as witnesses were describing his torture of civilians, was the only one of the three who showed signs of nervousness, crying 'goodbye forever' as he went to the gallows.

The execution of the three Japanese was held in the utmost secrecy.

(*Sunderland Daily Echo and Shipping Gazette*, Saturday, 23 February 1946)

At every village in a journey of 500 miles from the south to the north, I found Malays with banners and slogans and all the trappings of a Hyde Park meeting.

But the most remarkable thing is the part that women are playing. In the 14 years I lived in Malaya I hardly spoke to a Malay woman, but today young unmarried women get up and make speeches through microphones which would disgrace nobody in this house.

The whole business has gone into the emotional field, and reason in these circumstances can go out of the window. The first stage in settling their problems is for the MacMichael Treaties [enforcing the Malayan Union] to go.

Labour member Rees-Williams, however, contended that the solution to prevent civil unhappiness in Malaya lay with the Malays themselves. During their visit, he had attended a meeting at which about 7,000 Malays had come to discuss the British plan. Puzzled as to how such a large number of people came to be at the gathering, Rees-Williams was told, 'It was quite easy. The Army did it all for us.' The bemused MP had responded, 'Surely this is the one empire in the world where the Imperial Army would bring the rioters to the riot.'

British opinion over the Malaya question started to polarise between capitalist and liberal. One school endorsed Whitehall control of the peninsula's political and administrative machinery to safeguard rich resources instrumental to Britain's economic wellbeing. At the opposite end of the spectrum of British politics was the lobby that defended the right of self-determination of the peoples of Britain's far-flung colonies.

The tempo of nationalist fervour in Malaya increased. Sovereignty was being demanded, but a severance with Britain meant different things to different ethnic groups, primarily divided along ideological lines. Ethnic Malays desired a return to the archaic conglomerate of autonomous sultan states, whereas the ethnic Chinese propounded a red revolution based entirely on the Communist teachings of Mao Zedong.

The means of production, and therefore national wealth, was vested in the populace – London-based multi-nationals would be evicted by force. The Communist terrorist had a job to do.

Chairman Mao's 'Little Red Book', the Chinese Communist revolutionary's bible.

4. A CALL TO ARMS

BRITISH TROOPS FIGHT BANDITS IN MALAYA

Troops of the Dorsetshire Regiment using machine guns today aided Malayan police in a dawn action against Chinese gangsters. The Chinese had attacked police at Nyor village, five miles from Lluang, in Jahore State. Two gangsters were killed and five wounded. A British sergeant was injured by a hand grenade.

(Dundee Evening Telegraph, Thursday, 25 September 1947)

This brief, four-sentence report was easily missed in many newspapers in the UK. As much space was given in the British press to a report from American General Douglas MacArthur's headquarters, which stated that the wartime Pacific commander had ordered the return to Singapore's museum of 185 stuffed birds that the Japanese had pilfered during their occupation of Malaya for presentation to Emperor Hirohito.

The following month, the Chinese Chamber of Commerce, together with extreme left-wing parties, called for a *hartàl* – a general strike and closure of shops – in protest against plans by London to replace the unpopular Malayan Union with a federation of all the Malay states and Straits Settlements, but excluding Singapore.

Unperturbed, it was Britain's wish that 'internal self-government' be returned to the Malayan Peninsula, apart from the Crown Colony of Singapore. On 21 January 1948, Britain signed agreements in Kuala Lumpur with the rulers of nine Malayan states, thereby paving the way for a 'Federation of Malaya'. The new state would be promulgated by the issue of an Order in Council from Governor Sir Edward Gent in February. Gent would then become High Commissioner, while resident British commissioners in each of the federal states would only have advisory powers.

The latest British initiative merely served to harden Malayan Communist Chinese resolve to expedite their quest for a people's republic encompassing the whole peninsula.

While the wartime marriage of convenience between the British and the MCP's military wing, MPAJA, was a tactical necessity to rid Malaya of the Japanese, the MCP was already planning its strategies to also oust the British. A covert programme of Communist indoctrination by means of propaganda was conducted to sensitise the 'masses' to the need for resistance.

The MCP, however, could not anticipate the militarily strong British administration that took over from the Japanese, effectively stalling the timing of their revolution. While ensuring that they were seen by the British to be cooperative subjects of the Crown, the MCP took its subversive activities underground. In line with Mao's teachings, MCP activists infiltrated government and public departments, such as schooling and local government councils.

In the first quarter of 1948, the MCP started to implement by deed their doctrinal objectives. Initially, this took the form of nationwide civil disorder, exploiting the legitimacy of their actions in terms of the federal government's Trade Union Ordinance.

By this time, the MCP had divided its strategies into two – the Jungle Organisation and the Open Organisation. Whilst the federal authorities, 'assisted' by the British, were unable to

INDEFENSIBLE SINGAPORE NOW ONLY A POLICE POST

The great pre-war £26,000,000 Singapore naval base at Seletar has now been almost completely restored and is working at 80 or 90 per cent of its pre-war planned capacity. In additional to naval staff, 550 British civilians and 9,000 Asiatics are engaged on ship maintenance and repair.

But the once mighty 'fortress' of Singapore is no more. The 15-inch guns which 'pointed the wrong way' have been hacked into scrap and litter weed-covered emplacements, which the jungle is rapidly reclaiming.

The Second World War taught the lesson that Singapore Island, with its base, is indefensible unless a major front can be defended on the Malayan Peninsula or farther north.

Singapore, therefore, is finished as a great Empire bastion. But because of its location and the stabilising influence of British rule, it has become instead an important ' police station' in troubled Southeast Asia.

Now headquarters for British forces in the Far East, Singapore's depleted garrison still has sufficient forces, if needed, to ensure internal security in Malaya, Hong Kong, Ceylon, or neighbouring British islands.

A senior officer, discussing Singapore's place in Anglo-American strategy in any future war against Russia, said it could never be more than an advance repair station.

Airfields dot the peninsula from Penang to Singapore. But the Royal Air Force is now mainly interested in Singapore Island as a bomber and reconnaissance base. A fine runway has been built at Tengah, 12 miles north of Singapore, the only one in Malaya capable of taking Constellation aircraft – or new heavy bombers.

So today the British Empire possesses a magnificent naval base. A magnificent anchorage, it has 14 miles of water deep enough to take any ship and not too deep to prevent anchoring, closed at one end by the Johore causeway and neither tidal nor affected by wind. But – it is in the wrong place.

(*Western Morning News*, Monday, 26 January 1948)

---

legitimately classify the overt trade union activities as acts of terrorism, the Open Organisation played a fundamental role in the Communist insurrection.

The Jungle Organisation itself comprised two elements – the Malayan Races Liberation Army (MRLA) and the Min Yuen, or Mass People's Movement.

Initially comprised of regiments, logistical necessities made the structure difficult to manage, so independent platoons were created instead. With platoon strengths fluctuating between fifteen and thirty, the units came under the command of a state committee member (SCM), which allowed for areas of operation to overlap. Local militia, referred to as the Armed Work Force, augmented platoon ranks.

About 90 per cent of the communist terrorists were ethnic Chinese, the balance mainly Malay and Indian, with one or two Siamese, Japanese and Javanese. Generally young, the CTs were jungle habituated, attuned to the lay of the land in which they operated. Hardened

Headline from *The Press and Journal*, 13 January 1948.

survivalists, they understood deprivation and the necessity of living off the jungle. Their fieldcraft and tracking skills were, for the majority, second nature in the familiar environment.

Much of the CTs' war materiel, unearthed from Second World War jungle caches, was of diminished quality. Compounded by the metal-unfriendly jungle conditions, British military analysts rated CT handling and maintenance of arms and ammunition as 'adequate for the type of warfare they are engaged in'. Questionable weapons' serviceability impacted on the morale of the guerrillas. This, together with the efficacy of the British and Commonwealth security forces, food supply, quality of leadership and strength of conviction to the cause, meant for CT tactics that were largely hit-and-run in execution. Only the most zealous adherents to the Communist dogma would show determined resistance in combat.

The CTs drew from cached British and American stock weaponry issued to the anti-Japanese guerrillas during the occupation. Weapons included .303-calibre Bren light machine guns, 9mm Sten sub-machine guns, Thompson .45-calibre 'Chicago Organ Grinder' sub-machine guns, American .30 semi-automatic carbines, British .303 SMLE rifles, 12-bore shotguns, Russian-made Tokarev TT-33 pistols, and dated British revolvers.

CT campsites were meticulously selected, with an emphasis placed on unlikely positions to the casual observer, and a reliable source of clean water. The larger, more permanent camps had bashas constructed from natural materials found in the area, a parade ground and an outdoor lecture facility. Some camps had rudimentary armouries for basic weapons repair.

Two-way radio communications were rare, the CTs lacking suitable equipment. Two- or three-man courier groups were the norm in jungle operational areas, which included the conveyance of printed Communist propaganda. So-called open couriers proved the most effective and expedient means of communication, and one that the local law enforcement agencies found extremely difficult to detect, let alone eliminate. Invariably, these open couriers

A Ho Lung CT camp in the Sungei Palong area, southern Malaya. (Courtesy Brigadier John 'Digger' Essex-Clark)

were readily available Min Yuen, blending in with the general populace as an ordinary citizen going about their daily routines.

Instructional material in guerrilla tactics such as vehicle and security force ambushes, defensive positions, reconnaissance and use of weapons, was sourced from translations of Russian and British manuals, and leaflets of the Chinese People's Army sent in from China.

The Malayan civil government was, in the first instance, the responsible authority for the anti-terrorist campaign. Viewed at first as a civil action, CT attacks on civilians were regarded as of a criminal nature, and therefore a matter for the police force to address. With the escalation in acts of terrorism, armed forces – local, British and Commonwealth – were brought in to support the civil authorities. A home guard was also formed, mainly to release combatant troops from urban and village defence duties.

By 1950, the coordinated responsibility for the control of all counter-terrorist operations lay with the Emergency Operations Council – EOC. Answerable in turn to the federal government of Malaya, the EOC was tasked with the use of fully integrated civil and military resources to totally eradicate the Communist terrorists.

Chaired by the prime minister, the EOC comprised government ministers, the commissioner of police, the flag officer (navy) of the Malayan area, the general officer commanding overseas Commonwealth land forces, the air officer commanding No. 224 Group, RAF, and the deputy secretary, security and intelligence in the prime minister's office.

Responsible for the day-to-day conduct of emergency operations, the Federal Director of Emergency Operations was a senior British army officer seconded to the Federation of Malaya government. Generally referred to as the Director of Operations, this officer chaired the

BRITISH JUNGLE ARMY READY SOON

Kuala Lumpur, Thursday.

Britain's new offensive against the Malaya terrorists – special jungle squads – will be in the field soon, Mr Malcolm MacDonald, Commissioner General for South East Asia, told a conference of Chinese leaders here last night.

The squads had been training for the last few weeks to 'fight the enemy inside the jungle and kill him in his lair,' he said. 'From outside Malaya we are going to get whatever reinforcements are necessary to do the job quickly and completely.'

Meanwhile, as RAF planes continue to drop pamphlets throughout Malaya, Communists have intensified their propaganda warfare. Kluang police station in Johore yesterday received a bundle of Communist leaflets saying 'Down with the British' and promising 'Death for the running dogs of the British'.

Malaya today officially asked the British government for shotguns to replace and supplement rifles issued to newly recruited special constables guarding the estates and mines, it was learned through authoritative government sources.

(*Gloucester Citizen*, Thursday, 29 July 1948)

Commanders' Sub-committee, made up of the commanders of the army, air force, navy and police in Malaya. These combined forces' operational structures were replicated at state and district levels, in descending chain of command.

The job of the security forces was threefold:

1. The strict control of concentrations of the civilian population, in cities, towns, *kampongs* (villages) and plantation lines. The forces had to be in a position to not only defend civilians from CT intimidation and brutality, but also to prevent supplies of food being smuggled out to the CTs by Communist sympathisers.
2. To perform offensive operations in areas surrounding centres of population, with the objective of cutting the flow of food by eliminating the CTs.
3. To mount deep-jungle, seek-and-destroy missions to isolate them from the local populace and to destroy camps, food and arms caches, and lands cultivated for food production.

Severing the link between CT and civilian was deemed key, and therefore warranting a systematic programme of isolation of one from the other. This process became a reality with the controversial introduction of the Briggs Plan, looked at later in the book.

The Malayan federal police force command structure was also decentralised at the state level, with the national headquarters and commissioner in the capital. In addition to the regular uniform and detective branches, temporary and volunteer police included special constables, temporary female searchers, a special operational volunteer force, and a police volunteer reserve.

The Special Constabulary and Police Field Force were primarily raised, trained and equipped to perform para-military duties along the same lines as the army. The latter were specifically deployed to protect jungle forts, and to conduct cross-border operations into neighbouring

Five special constables on escort duty in the back of an armoured short-wheel-base Land Rover. (Courtesy John Anderson)

Siam. The force also included trained riot squads. The Special Constabulary was formed into Area Security Units (SU) and Police Special Squads (PSS), tasked with conducting offensive operations in developed areas, the enforcement of food-movement restriction measures, and the guarding of planters, miners and utility installations.

In combined operations rooms, the vitally important monitoring and plotting of army and police unit positions were conducted. The police were required to retain their non-military police functions of protecting civilian life and property from the army. To this end, airstrikes called in by army units had to be cleared by the resident police commander.

The role of the army was also twofold. The primary role was to seek, flush out and destroy the CTs in the jungles and immediate surrounding areas. A secondary role was in support of the federal police in their tasks to enforce food-restriction measures, curfews, roadblocks, and static stop-and-search posts.

Depending on the magnitude of CT activity in a state, army deployments paralleled that of the police at the state and district levels. The upper echelons of the army were headquartered in state capitals, alongside the police contingent headquarters. Below these were battalions or brigades in the administrative centre of the civil district, and then infantry companies in each police district.

The standard company platoon of conventional warfare had to be adapted to accommodate the idiosyncrasies of Malayan terrain and jungle. The Communist terrorist, unencumbered by weighty arms and equipment, was able to move with some speed in the jungle. The platoon model contained in army handbooks on anti-terrorist operations during the Malayan emergency, comprised a platoon commander and his assistant, a platoon sergeant or warrant officer. The platoon itself would be made up of a reconnaissance group, including scouts, a

An RhAR section, armed with a miscellany of .303 SMLE jungle carbines, an American-made M2, a Sterling sub-machine gun and a Bren machine gun. (Courtesy Brigadier John 'Digger' Essex-Clark)

support group with two light-machine-gun operators, and a rifle group of soldiers with firearms. An NCO would be in command of each group. Specialists might also be attached to a platoon, such as a medic, police officer, translator or guide.

The platoon's weaponry, particularly that of the rifleman, was replaced with more advanced firearms during the twelve-year emergency as global arms manufacturers vied with each other to produce technically superior weapons. For the most part, however, security forces were issued with a miscellany of Second World War firearms. These included:

1. The single-shot Lee Enfield No. 5 rifle, a derivative of the No. 4 Mk I. With a magazine capacity of ten .303 rounds, the bolt-action rifle was four inches shorter and more than two pounds lighter than the No. 4. With its diagnostic conical flash eliminator and 'custom design', it earned the sobriquet 'jungle carbine' from the security forces serving in the Malayan Emergency.
2. With time, the No. 5 rifle was replaced with the advanced self-loading rifle, FN FAL. Manufactured by Fabrique Nationale in Belgium, the 7.62mm-calibre battle rifle carried a twenty-round magazine. In Malaya, the rifle was set to semi-automatic fire only, the pistol grip making for much-improved accuracy.
3. The reliable stalwart of Second World War infantry, the .303 Bren light machine gun, continued to deliver in Malaya. The Bren, with its characteristic forward-curved magazine, was the weapon feared most by CTs.

WHY ME? I'VE HAD MY WAR

Must we have a Territorial Army?

No, but we'd be fools to ignore the possibility.

All right. Suppose there was a war. Wouldn't it be a push-button affair, all over before you could say 'Right turn?'

We don't know. All we know is that we might be called upon to defend this island.

What with? We can't shoot down rockets with rifles.

Rockets aren't the only means of attack – and rifles aren't the only means of defence. Our boffins haven't been busy in their back rooms for nothing.

You mean we need a Territorial Army to operate new defence weapons?

If ever the time comes – yes. The point is, we can't wait. We must start training now.

O.K. But what's that to me? I've had my war. The National Service men are serving 6 years as 'Terriers' after their demob, aren't they?

That's just the point. We need men who've seen service and know the ropes to give these youngsters a lead. A foundation of 'seasoned' men, men they can look up to, will make all the difference.

Maybe. And what do we get out of it?

Quite frankly, very little – apart from a maximum bounty of £12 and the satisfaction of giving up some of your spare time to something of real national importance.

H'mm. How much spare time?

To qualify for the full bounty, a minimum of 44 two-hour training periods during the year, plus 8 days in camp. But there are various ways you can put in the time according to your circumstances. The C.O. of your local unit will be glad to see you and give you all the gen. Why not go and see him?

Spare time for Britain in the Territorial Army. Take the lead – join your local unit now.

(Territorial Army recruitment drive. *Aberdeen Journal*, Saturday, 9 October 1948)

4. The American M1 and M2 Garand .30-calibre carbines remained the federal Malay forces' attack rifle after British and Commonwealth forces converted to the FN FAL. Unlike the M1, the M2 had a selective-fire capability to allow for fully automatic fire.

5. Nicknamed the 'Digger's Darling', the 9mm Owen machine carbine was designed in Australia, and remained that nation's army's main sub-machine gun from 1943 until the mid-1960s. Of robust and relatively cheap construction, the Owen, with its gravity-fed, top-mounted, thirty-three round magazine, was popular amongst British troops in the jungle.

6. The other sub-machine gun used in the emergency was the Patchett carbine, more commonly known as the Sterling. Similar to the Sten in many ways, the 9mm Sterling was a favoured weapon for the New Zealand and Australian SAS.

Lieutenant Essex-Clark, standing centre, with platoon leaders, armed with an 7.62mm SLR, .303 SMLE jungle carbines, M2 rifles, Sterling sub-machine guns and a Bren machine gun. (Courtesy Brigadier John 'Digger' Essex-Clark)

7. Remington pump-action and Browning semi-automatic 12-bore shotguns were often carried by a platoon as an effective weapon in restricted jungle-combat conditions.
8. The use of mortars in the jungle was both impractical and dangerous. In lieu of this, modified Lee Enfield rifles were fitted with a cup and a base plate from which a Mills-36 grenade could be fired into enemy positions, using a special blank (ballistite) cartridge. The weapons were referred to as GF – grenade-firing – rifles.

Some forty British army infantry regiments performed tours of duty in the twelve years of the emergency, plus seven partly formed Gurkha regiments. These numbers were augmented with locally raised units, including thirteen battalions of the Malayan Regiment and two of the Royal Malay Regiment.

Specialist operational support came from the Special Air Service (SAS), the Commandos, the Royal Marines and the Independent Parachute Squadron, and field regiments of the Royal Artillery. To complete the British order of battle, were elements of the Royal, Gurkha and Malayan Engineers, Signals, and the Royal Army Service Corps.

Commonwealth troop contributions were significant:

Australia – 1st, 2nd and 3rd battalions, The Royal Australian Regiment.
Fiji – 1st, Battalion Fiji Infantry Regiment.

Kingdom of Sarawak, Borneo – the Sarawak Rangers.

New Zealand – New Zealand Squadron, Special Air Service, and 1st and 2nd battalions, The New Zealand Regiment.

Northern Rhodesia – The Northern Rhodesia Regiment.

Nyasaland – 2nd (Nyasaland) Battalion, The King's African Rifles.

Southern Rhodesia – 1st Battalion, The Rhodesian African Rifles, and C Squadron, Special Air Service (formerly the Southern Rhodesia Far East Volunteer Unit)

The original '100', Rhodesian C Squadron, SAS, in Malaya, 1953. (Courtesy Craig Fourie)

Malaya bound. Senior NCOs of the 1st Battalion, The Rhodesian African Rifles (RhAR). (Courtesy Rhodesian African Rifles Regimental Association (UK))

Left: RhAR troops undergo intensive training before departing for Malaya. (Courtesy Rhodesian African Rifles Regimental Association (UK))

Below: An RhAR warrant officer, armed with a Sterling submachine gun, scans his front. (Courtesy Rhodesian African Rifles Regimental Association (UK))

The Royal Air Force (RAF) and Army Air Corps, based in Malaya, provided multi-role air support to emergency operations. This was either as an independent force of the operation, or in direct cooperation with forces on the ground. There were six facets to the availability of air support:

1. Photographic air reconnaissance facilitated informed planning and execution of anti-terrorist operations. An extensive air survey was conducted of the heavily populated areas, and active photographic tactical air cover made available. Light fixed-wing aircraft of the Army Air Corps were used for routine visual air reconnaissance, and had an active role target marking for RAF airstrikes.
2. Offensive air support was also multi-role. Due to restricted ground visibility from the air because of the very thick jungle canopy, the RAF had to rely heavily on pinpoint target coordinates from the ground forces for airstrikes to be effective. In the event of targets covering an extended area, but also dependent on target identification from the ground, bombers could lay down a deadly pattern to neutralise guerrillas positions. Often, an RAF representative would participate in the planning and implementation of ground operations in an advisory capacity when air support was included.
3. The supply of rations, ammunition and general supplies was essential to maintain sustained jungle operations. The terrain and general absence of a serviceable road network made the role of air supply critical for the success of prolonged counter-insurgency operations in the Malayan jungles.

SHANGHAI STUDENTS PROTEST

The United States and Britain were denounced when 10,000 students of both sexes staged a demonstration today outside the British Consulate in Shanghai in protest against the Kowloon evictions.

They dispersed after a small deputation had been permitted to present a petition to the British Consul-General. While being escorted inside the compound, a member of the deputation, bearing a Chinese flag, ran towards a flagpole on which the Union Jack was flying, but he was stopped by police.

Five-hundred police, armed with tommy-guns and rifles and supported by three armoured cars, maintained order within an area of less than a square mile throughout the demonstration.

The students presented an 'ultimatum' which ended with a warning that if no reply to their petition was forthcoming from the British authorities within one week, students and other Chinese would adopt the same 'spirit as displayed against Japanese aggression'.

The wall of the British consulate were covered with slogans such as: Down with British and U.S. Imperialism', We must fight to the last ditch to regain Hong Kong and Kowloon'. 'Get out of China, British and US Army'.

(*Hartlepool Northern Daily Mail*, Saturday, 17 January 1948)

4. For the same reasons, inaccessible areas of jungle required deployment of troops by air – light aircraft and medium helicopters. It also allowed for improved effectiveness as the troops could be deployed quicker and closer to the enemy.

5. Casualty evacuation by helicopter saved the lives of many a soldier wounded in action or suffering from some debilitating tropical disease. The medical exfiltration by this means enabled ground troops to continue with their operations, rather than having to evacuate a casualty by foot.

6. The dissemination of anti-Communist propaganda by air was also deemed useful, although problematic to quantify in absolute terms. Aerial leaflet drops or voice broadcasts formed an integral part of the psychological warfare during the emergency.

Around twenty squadrons from Britain's Far East Air Force served during the emergency, flying English Electric Canberra bomber and reconnaissance aircraft, Spitfire FR-18s and -19s, Beaufighter TF-10s, de Havilland Mosquitos, Vampires and Venoms, Gloster Meteors, Percival Pembrokes, Scottish Aviation Pioneers, Taylorcraft Austers, Sunderlands Mk Vs (RAF Kai Tak, Hong Kong, and RAF Seletar, Singapore), Avro Lincolns, Westland Whirlwind helicopters, Bristol Sycamores, Douglas Dakotas, Vickers Valettas and Sikorsky helicopters.

The Royal Australian Air Force squadrons contributed Avro Lincoln heavy bombers (Butterworth air base), Canberra bombers, Dakota transports and CAC Sabre jet fighters; and from the Royal New Zealand Air Force, Vampires, Venoms, Dakotas, Bristol Freighters and Canberras.

Ships from the Royal Navy, such as HMS *Amethyst*, *Comus*, *Defender*, *Hart*, *Newcastle* and *Newfoundland*, conducted coastal anti-smuggling and anti-piracy operations, and were used for amphibious landings into inaccessible areas near the coast. Naval vessels also provided bombardment of targeted CT areas.

Naval support also came from Australia – destroyers *Warramunga* and *Arunta*, aircraft carriers *Melbourne* and *Sydney*, and Commonwealth Strategic Reserve forces destroyers *Anzac*, *Quadrant*, *Queenborough*, *Quiberon*, *Quickmatch*, *Tobruk*, *Vampire*, *Vendetta* and *Voyager*. The Royal New Zealand Navy's frigate, HMNZS *Pukaki* complemented coastal patrols.

An RAF Bristol Sycamore HR14 picks up South Wales Borderers handlers and their tracker dogs. (Courtesy Rhodesian African Rifles Regimental Association (UK))

5. ISOLATE AND FLUSH OUT

At the time of the emergency, four-fifths of the Malayan peninsula was covered in predominantly virgin jungle and swamps, providing ideal terrain for guerrilla warfare. Heavily forested mountains run along the central spine of the country, from which fast-flowing rivers cascade to the sea, providing the only means of communication in many areas.

Service roads supporting the north–south rail link from Singapore to Bangkok in Siam were of a good standard, but the feeder roads to the rubber plantations and tin mines were generally inferior. The Communist terrorists – CTs – were able to select ambush spots along these roads with a large element of impunity, disappearing into the jungle and swamps after they had sprung an ambush.

Post-war British Malaya remained ethnically diverse. The indigenous Sakai numbered around 100,000, although they largely comprised groups of mixed races. As natives of the jungles, the Sakai were therefore the CTs' couriers, guides and scouts of choice.

MALAYA APPOINTS ANTI-REBEL CHIEF

Biggest move yet in the anti-bandit campaign in Malaya was taken today by the appointment of Lieut.-General Sir Harold Rawdon Briggs as virtual dictator of all the security forces in the state, says a message from Kuala Lumpur.

Meanwhile rebel outrages continue. Reports from Singapore today state that a number of people have been killed and others injured in further terrorist attacks.

Lieut.-General Briggs will be responsible for planning, coordinating, and directing anti-bandit operations in consultation with the chiefs of the various components of the security forces. An official announcement stated that General Briggs's primary function would be to secure full and effective coordination. He will allocate tasks to the various forces and decide priorities of these tasks and their general timing and sequence.

General Briggs, who is 55, was General Officer Commanding-in-Chief, Burma Command from 1946 until January, 1948.

He commanded the 7th Indian Infantry Brigade in Eritrea and the Western Desert from 1940 to 1942, and the Fifth Indian Division in the Western Desert, Iraq and Burma from 1942 to 1944.

During the war, General Briggs was awarded the D.S.O. and two bars for exceptional performances while commanding the 7th Indian Infantry Brigade, and for gallantry in Arakan.

He was born in Minnesota, U.S.A. and came to England when he was very young.

General Briggs, who retired from the Army in 1948, is expected in Malaya shortly to take up his new post – a civil appointment.

(*Gloucestershire Echo*, Tuesday, 21 March 1950)

The dense Malayan jungle. (Courtesy Rhodesian African Rifles Regimental Association (UK))

An indigenous riverbank settlement, where transport is by river only. (Courtesy Rhodesian African Rifles Regimental Association (UK))

The hereditary rulers and Malays were of Sumatran origin, and numbered almost 2,500,000. Agriculturalist and Muslim, the Malays were staunchly loyal to their sultan rulers.

Rapidly gaining numerical superiority on the peninsula, however, were the Chinese. Two-thirds were born in China, with which they maintained strong links, shunning any form of Malayan assimilation. With a significant stake in the rubber and tin enterprises, the resident Chinese adhered to their own codes of living and Chinese dialects; interaction by the colonial administration was therefore, more often than not, problematic.

A final substantial ethnic group was the Indians, dominated by Tamils.

For the insurgent, predominantly Chinese CTs, support and succour from the large ethnic-Chinese population, especially in rural areas, was a virtual certainty. Early on, it was recognised that a diversity of administrative, police and military resources would have to be employed to initially deny the CTs access to the rural populace. This would isolate the guerrillas, allowing the security forces to implement and execute far more effective counter-terrorist operations.

The British administration's strategy to achieve these objectives essentially comprised two interlinked elements: 1. the restriction and prohibition of foodstuffs and other supplies, as promulgated in emergency regulations; and 2. The optimisation of administrative control of the nation's total population.

The definition of foodstuffs ranged from any live or dead animal, to stock feeds such as rice bran. Restricted articles included cooked, tinned or dried foodstuffs, such as *padi* – unmilled rice – flour, oil, sugar, salt and fish. Other restricted articles included paper and printing ink, medicines, torches and batteries, canvas articles, green or khaki cloth, and pliable plastic or rubberised material. The movement out of a Restricted Food Area included fresh foods, such as meat, fish, eggs, tapioca, poultry, fruit and shellfish. 'Ice cream, cordial or beverages containing less than 15% sugar' were also exempt.

In 1950, British General Sir Harold Briggs was appointed Director of Operations in Malaya. Shortly afterwards, he introduced a radical and controversial 'New Villages' plan aimed at a forced resettlement in rural areas of about 10 per cent of the Malayan population. In later years, Briggs's model of isolation of a rural population would be emulated by Portugal in her African colonies, *aldeamentos*, and by the widespread construction of protected villages by the Rhodesian government during that country's anti-terrorist war of the 1970s.

The retired Lieutenant General Sir Rawdon Briggs KCIE, KBE, CB, DSO and two bars, was a Second World War veteran of the Western Desert, East Africa, Persia and Burma theatres of war. In 1950, Briggs was approached by former Allied Land Forces South East Asia commander, Field Marshal William 'Bill' Slim, to assume command of operations in Malaya. Slim, destined to become the thirteenth Governor General of Australia, held Briggs in high esteem, reportedly saying, 'I know of few commanders who made as many immediate and critical decisions on every step of the ladder of promotion, and I know of none who made so few mistakes.'

A year after his appointment, his health ailing, Briggs retired once more to Cyprus where he passed away in 1952. On 22 January 1952, Winston Churchill appointed General Sir Gerald Walter Robert Templer KCB, GCMG, KBE, DSO, High Commissioner in Malaya to tackle the emergency. The continued development of the eponymous Briggs Plan was a priority.

It was estimated at the time that over half a million Chinese 'squatters' lived in scattered, often isolated places on the peninsula. These had to be uprooted en masse and resettled in

Lieutenant General Sir Rawdon Briggs KCIE, KBE, CB, DSO & Two Bars, seen here in Burma during the Second World War. (Source *The War Illustrated*)

new villages established expressly to secure administration and protection away from CT influences and subversion through intimidation.

In an unprecedented social experiment in the history of British colonial administration, young district officers and army subalterns were given the task of the physical implementation of the plan on the ground.

The villages were enclosed with security fencing, where the inhabitants came under the authority and protection of the police and military. Those resettled in this manner were documented and encouraged to participate in the election and running of their own village councils. Educational, health and trading facilities formed integral and important necessities

Jungle clearing to accommodate a 'New Village'. (Courtesy John Anderson)

for the creation and sustainability of community cohesiveness. Political indoctrination in villages schools, however, was virtually impossible to assess, let alone control – Chinese-speaking inspectors were extremely rare.

Former planter John Anderson comments:

Oh blimey, I had one [New Village] just a mile or two from me. When they were being set up, of course, the Communists used to attack them. So I had a few sleepless nights of people shooting each other – but not me.

The people that were moved into them were moved largely from the fringes of the estates, where they could work, have a bit of a garden – grow their own stuff. They were considerably upset about having to abandon their homes.

The state tappers did not stay in the new villages. The estate provided the lines [accommodation], a hospital, a school, and all that sort of thing. The lines were surrounded by barbed-wire fences and patrolled by special constables. Part of the rubber factory had been converted into accommodation for these guards.

When I arrived, they were being paid $2.40 a day [this was the Malayan dollar, which was later replaced with the ringgit].

By the time I left – I left thirty years ago – the new villages were established townships.

When you had food, you were never allowed to travel on your own. The idea was to starve the terrorists out. We used to have central cooking on the estate. We used to cook the rice, while the labourers, clerks and everybody could cook their own meat or whatever to go with the rice. It worked quite well, and as I said, I had to arrange and account for food.

For the ground troops in Malaya, the first few weeks after arrival was a period of acclimatisation and adaptation. For most, especially the British and Commonwealth troops, the unforgiving jungle environment was very alien.

ILL-ARMED BANDITS CHALLENGE BRITISH TROOPS

The situation in Malaya was described as fantastic by Mr L.D. Gammans (C., Hornsey) in the House of Commons today. Three or four thousand ill-armed bandits were challenging with impunity very nearly a division of British troops and 50,000 police, he said.

The situation was grave and was getting worse instead of better.

'Malaya has just had an anti-bandit month. There was great response from the civil population which proves that this is in no sense a Nationalist uprising, but the results have been disappointing in the extreme.

'On the whole the bandits have killed nearly twice as many people of the security forces as we killed – 77 members of the security forces as against 38 bandits.'

Mr Gammans read a letter from a planter's wife which stated: 'We sleep with a Sten gun under our bed and a revolver in bed, and if we go anywhere at all the last thing to go into the car are the gun and the baby's rattle. The baby appears to be cutting her teeth on the revolver'.

'Yet,' said Mr Gammans, 'these people carry on month after month.'

Mr Gammans said of our recognition of Communist China, 'Is there any wonder, now that the Communist regime in Peking is recognised, that the Chinese in Malaya look over their shoulders and wonder who is going to control Malaya in a few years?'

'This is not a Nationalistic uprising, it is a war, and the only way to win a war is to fight it out.

'We have to admit that the present type of military and police action has very largely failed. One of the reasons has been that we have been compelled to use short-term national service troops for a job for which they were never intended.'

Has any approach been made for help to Australia and New Zealand? If Singapore fell, Australia and New Zealand would be in the most deadly peril.

During the last half of 1949, there was every indication that we were steadily getting on top of the bandits. Since, however, the attacks had increased to about 50, or, at the peak, to 60 a week.

'Additional aircraft are being sent, including Lincoln squadrons from the U.K.'

Mr James Griffiths, Colonial Secretary ... said that the possibility of assistance from other Commonwealth sources had not been overlooked.

(*Gloucestershire Echo*, Thursday, 6 April 1950)

The rigours of prolonged periods seeking out an impossibly elusive enemy imposed the need to allow the 'working' environment to dictate the manner in which operations were conducted.

The intense heat and humidity of the theatre of operations, combined with the restrictive confines of the dense jungle, led to more practical patrol methodology and field operations evolving that were not necessarily of military handbook origin.

Retired Brigadier John 'Digger' Essex-Clark, a long-serving veteran of the Australian army, was a young subaltern when he first arrived in Malaya with the Rhodesian African Rifles. 'Digger', who attended the British Army Staff College in 1963, subsequently joined the Australian army, which included a tour of duty with the Royal Australian Regiment in Vietnam in the mid-1960s. He relates how the Malayan experience honed the skills of many an infantryman:

'Digger' Essex-Clark with a recently issued 7.62mm SLR automatic rifle, 1957. (Courtesy Brigadier John 'Digger' Essex-Clark)

One of the major problems for any infantryman is his load. He carries everything he needs both to live and to fight and has his home on his back. But the greater the load and the longer it is carried, the less able he is to fight.

In 1957, I'd changed to a SLR 7.62mm self-loading rifle, so I now had an all-up load of 42 kilograms which was just under half my body weight. I was putting 133 kilos on each foot as I walked and some of my askaris carried more than I did. We were expected to be able to march for perhaps seven hours of the day with a ten-minute break every 50 minutes. Our march speed was in tempo with, say, 'Blueberry Hill' by Fats Domino.

But we threw away thirty percent of our rations, including roughage such as the oatmeal block and dog biscuits. This particular load did not help our health in later life. We stripped away every item we could, including the metal buckles from our trousers. I had lightened our three Bren guns by taking off the back sight and foresight, and magazine opening cover, but added a pistol grip for the left hand. My prismatic compass was unrecognisable as I needed only the needle to point north and the rotating bevel for rough direction.

Our two routine periods of the day were evenings and dawn stand-to, when we were supposed to be the most vulnerable. However, most CTs – trained by the British for the Malayan People's Anti-Japanese Army eleven years before – would be standing to at the same time. Therefore, it was probably the safest period for both of us.

Nevertheless, the askaris had their rifles, shotguns, carbines or machine guns in hand, and checked the location of the 'buddy' groups of two men on their flanks. [Warrant Officer] Pisayi and I would move slowly around the perimeter, check weapons' cleanliness and sight settings, make sure each man knew where our sentries were and ensure that each askari did not neglect to take his anti-malarial pill.

I would also check the quality and safety of fields of fire for the Bren guns, check every sentry position and ensure that every group knew its job if we were attacked. I would also have a chat with each of my askaris. Often, when we were patrolling by sections, it would be the only time I could yarn with them. It was a good time to boost flagging spirits, note and remedy any unhappiness and get a feel for morale. My task was to get a smile from every soldier.

Stand-to in the evening ended just after last light and in the morning started just before first light. My definition of first and last light was the moment when you could, for the first time at dawn or last time at dusk, clearly see a stationary man in the sights of a rifle at twenty-five metres. We stood down when the sentries were in position, when the outer clearing patrols had returned and my sixth sense told me there was no immediate danger. There was no definite time for first or last light because it depended on the weather and the thickness of the foliage above and around us.

Some are fanatics about the care and maintenance of stores and weapons and I was one of them. I spent two days looking for a lost prismatic compass and finally found it. On one thundery day, we were crossing over a deep rushing stream on a log – tactically a stupid thing

RhAR soldier burdened with loaded Pattern 44 webbing and recovered parachute. (Courtesy Brigadier John 'Digger' Essex-Clark)

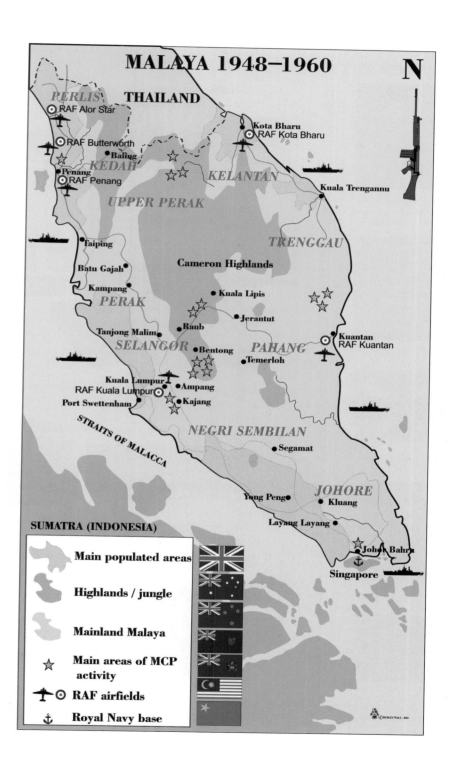

FORMATION FLASHES
MALAYAN EMERGENCY

HQ Overseas
Commonwealth Land Forces
based in Singapore

Malaya Command

17th Gurkha Division

17th Infantry Division

40th Infantry Division
Based in Hong Kong and supplied units
for deployment to Malay

EQUIPMENT USED IN THE MALAYA EMERGENCY

Ferret armoured car of 1st King's Dragoon Guards
deployed in the Mantin Pass

Saladin armoured car deployed in Malaya Emergency

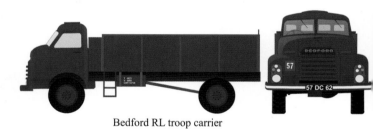

Bedford RL troop carrier

25 Pounder
A Troop, 75th Battery, 148th Field Regiment Royal Artillery
deployed in the Nembi Segrilan area

RAF AIRCRAFT IN THE MALAYA EMERGENCY

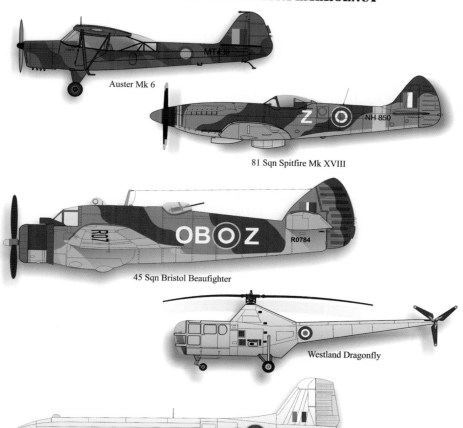

Auster Mk 6

81 Sqn Spitfire Mk XVIII

45 Sqn Bristol Beaufighter

Westland Dragonfly

209 Sqn Douglas DC-3 Dakota

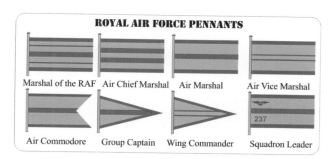

ROYAL AIR FORCE PENNANTS

Marshal of the RAF Air Chief Marshal Air Marshal Air Vice Marshal

Air Commodore Group Captain Wing Commander Squadron Leader

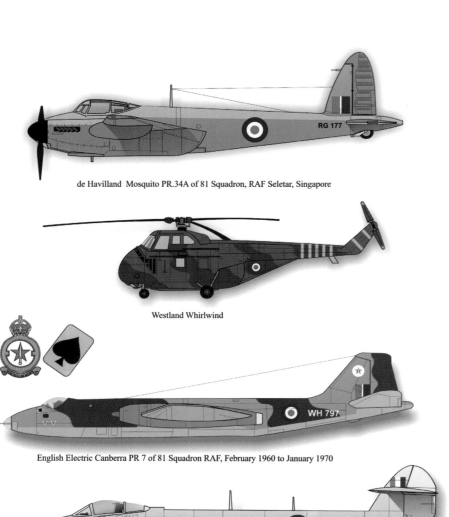

de Havilland Mosquito PR.34A of 81 Squadron, RAF Seletar, Singapore

Westland Whirlwind

English Electric Canberra PR 7 of 81 Squadron RAF, February 1960 to January 1970

Gloster Meteor PR Mk 10 of 81 Squadron RAF, January 1954 to July 1961

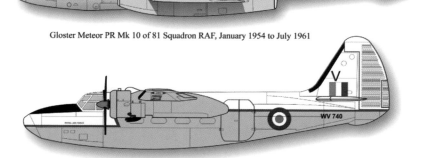

Hunting Percival Pembroke C (PR) Mk 1 of 81 Squadron RAF, January 1956 to July 1960

SMALL ARMS USED DURING THE MALAYA CAMPAIGN

.303 No. 4

.303 Jungle Carbine

US M2 .30 self-loading carbine

SLR 7.62 x 51mm

Sten gun 9mm

Sterling L2A3 9mm

Bren light machine gun .303

Smith and Wesson .38

Colt 1911 .45

SELECTION OF BRITISH FORCES IN THE MALAYA CAMPAIGN

1st King's Own Dragoon Guards
cap badge

Lt Col F. Walker
PWO West Yorks Regt

PWO West Yorkshire Regt
cap badge

Grenadier Guards

2nd Gurkha Rifles
slouch hat patch

Royal Hampshire Regt

2nd Gurkha Rifles
cap badge

Royal Marines
cap badge

Royal Navy
Chief Petty Officers
cap badge

Royal Artillery
other ranks
cap badge

Royal Engineers
other ranks
cap badge

Royal Air Force
other ranks
cap badge

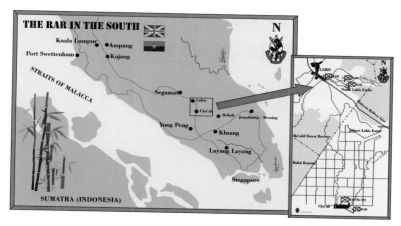

BADGES OF VARIOUS COLONIAL UNITS DEPLOYED TO MALAYA

Cap badge and shoulder title
Rhodesian African Rifles

Cap badge and shoulder title
1st Bn King's African Rifles

Cap badge and shoulder title
2nd Bn King's African Rifles

Cap badge and shoulder title
Northern Rhodesia Regiment

Badges
Malayan Scouts (SAS)

Hero and Veteran of the Malaya Campaign

WO 2 Pisayi Muzerecho, 1 RAR, was awarded the Military Medal for
bravery in Malaya. (see Chapter Six)
Painting by Captain Russell Fulton, (1 RAR) in 2016.

ENEMY STRATEGY AND TACTICS IN MALAYA

STAGES OF INSURGENCY

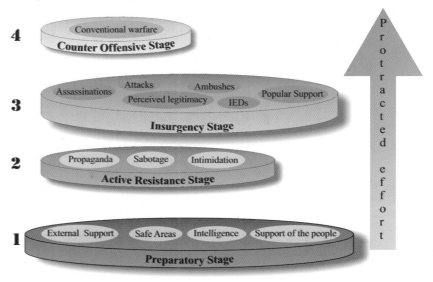

4 Conventional warfare
Counter Offensive Stage

3 Assassinations / Attacks / Ambushes / Perceived legitimacy / IEDs / Popular Support
Insurgency Stage

2 Propaganda / Sabotage / Intimidation
Active Resistance Stage

1 External Support / Safe Areas / Intelligence / Support of the people
Preparatory Stage

Protracted effort

METHODOLOGY

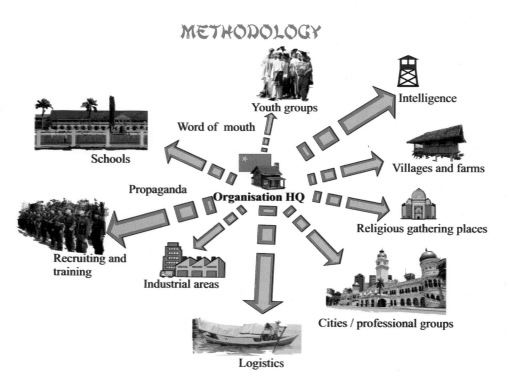

Youth groups
Word of mouth
Intelligence
Schools
Villages and farms
Propaganda
Organisation HQ
Religious gathering places
Recruiting and training
Industrial areas
Cities / professional groups
Logistics

BURMA-FAMED SUSSEX BATTALION DISBANDS IN MALAYA

Disbanded in Malaya this week was the 9th Battalion The Royal Sussex Regiment – veteran campaigner of Arakan and North Burma battles. The 9th was one of the line regiments of the famous British 26th Division that helped establish a new prestige for Britain's jungle fighters.

Flown into Myitkyina over the mountain barrier that separates India and Burma, the battalion was well to the fore in the fighting along the whole length of the Railway Corridor from Mogaung to Katha. The battalion shared the honour of being one of the British units fighting furthest from home and of having been supplied almost continuously from the air for one whole year. The whole of the Christmas donner came floating down out of the sky to the Sussex men taking a spell out of the lines over the festive season of 1944.

Since it arrived in Malaya last September, the battalion has been engaged on garrison duties in the famed 'Somerset Maughan' country of North Malaya. It played a very large part in the rounding up of Japs and the re-establishment of law and order.

Men of the unit made many friends among the civil population, both on the sports field and in the village halls where the battalion concert party entertained young and old Malayans alike. In fact it will be many years before the inhabitants of Butterworth and Bukit Mertajam forget 'Variety Pie, the 'R.S.s' own slap-happy venue.

(*Sussex Agricultural Express*, Friday, 5 April 1946)

to do but with non-swimming askaris you took the risk, and it was quicker. A Bren gunner fell in and panicked. I got the askari but he'd let go of his 9kg Bren gun. Impetuously, I dived down with a rope on my belt. The swirling muddy water made visibility less than a few centimetres, and there were bits of water-logged branches and muck swirling around and bumping me. I touched the bottom but panicked when I felt a vine tangling my ankle. I reached down to release myself – from the webbing sling of the lost Bren. The askaris laughed and cheered when I spluttered to the surface and held 'Excalibur' high above me. But I'd been a fool.

When we were out of the jungle and back in camp, we had the normal run of officer duties: orderly officer, escort to leave groups to our rest camp near Port Dickson, company commander's discipline of wayward soldiers and courts martial. The courts martial were both a test of intellect and light relief.

Zachariah, who had been with me on the Palong contact, was charged with an accidental discharge of his Bren during a night ambush in the rubber. Accidental discharges brought an automatic court martial because they endangered the lives of our own soldiers and, mostly, were due to carelessness. In this case, Zacka insisted that he had cocked the weapon carefully and quietly and was adjusting the tripod when it fired. No finger had been near the trigger and it had been on 'safe'. I asked to be his defending officer. I then spent two days on our range examining and firing Brens and Zacka's in particular.

At the court martial, a row of bemedalled senior British Army officers glowered at me. When I asserted that there was no case against the accused, there was consternation and

Above: Flooding, fast-flowing rivers were a common feature while on patrol in the jungle, and they had to be crossed. (Courtesy Rhodesian African Rifles Regimental Association (UK))

Left: Knee-deep mud for this Bren gunner. (Courtesy Rhodesian African Rifles Regimental Association (UK))

much twittering. I asked the court to come with me to the nearby jungle range where Pisayi and Gondo were looking after six loaded Brens on the firing point.

After the court assured themselves that the change lever on each weapon was on 'safe', 'repetition' or 'automatic', I asked them to stand back from the firing point and tapped each weapon on the bipod, magazine or butt. They all fired one single shot with not a finger near the trigger. Oohs and ahs abounded. I then explained the defect I had found in silent cocking, or when the weapon is cocked at the waist when a full pull-back of the cocking handle is difficult. Zacka's case was dismissed.

After that, throughout Malaya, silent cocking was allowed only if the magazine was placed on the weapon after it was cocked. I was rather pleased with myself. Not so my superiors, except Bill Godwin. They were still smarting from the time, after a contact in the jungle, that I had test-fired a freshly captured CT Sten gun and its ammunition and then been berated by my commanding officer because the ammunition might have been 'doctored' by Special Branch before delivery to the CT by turned Min Yuen. He was not happy with my reply that it would be sensible if we combat soldiers were warned of police activity that could endanger the lives of our own men. I felt over-zealous secrecy was stupid.

Perhaps for that sin I was sent later as an officer-under-instruction to other courts martial in British units. I was under the firm hand of Major 'Thank-you-kindly' Griffiths, the permanent president of courts martial in Malaya, and attended a series of bizarre cases, including a soldier who had whistled at a CT female in an ambush. There was another who had taken at his word his hut NCO who, when irritated by a thundering snorer in the hut, had said, 'I wish someone would shoot that man!' and a sentry who had accidentally shot the driver of a general's escort vehicle. I was glad to get back to my fairly predictable askaris and the serenity of the jungle. But it was a short step from that Lewis Carroll atmosphere to leaving Malaya. We left on the troopship *Dilwara* in February 1958.

The relative successes of the Briggs Plan determined that the gathering of intelligence took on new meaning. With the CTs' lifeline with the rural populace largely cut off, clandestine intelligence operations by the security forces were less hindered by the presence of civilians in CT-active areas.

The Special Branch of the Federal Police Force was the 'principal intelligence producing agency' during the emergency, responsible for the 'collection, collation and dissemination of intelligence relating to the MCP' – the Malayan Communist Party.

The Special Military Intelligence Staff (Malaya) was the security-force equivalent. Working in the Special Branch of the police force, specially trained military intelligence officers dealt with tactical intelligence and the order of battle of the MCP. In this complementary manner, Special Branch was the provider of intelligence and the army the operational user.

The respective 17th Gurkha Division, OCLF (Overseas Commonwealth Land Forces) and Federation Army headquarters each had their own intelligence staffs. These structures facilitated a military channel for the reporting of CT-related incidents and information from their own troops, working in close collaboration with Special Branch. This system, wherever possible, would be replicated at brigade and battalion levels, where intelligence staff jointly manned Contingent, Circle and Independent District Operations Rooms with the police. Such integration provided essential tactical information for military commanders to formulate day-to-day plans with confidence.

Battalion operations room, which included twenty-four-hour radio watch. (Courtesy Rhodesian African Rifles Regimental Association (UK))

GURKHAS SWITCHED FROM HONG-KONG TO MALAYA

British troops are to be transferred from Hong-Kong to Malaya to support the anti-terrorist campaign, Army headquarters announced in Hong-Kong today.

The announcement read: 'The 26th Gurkha Infantry Brigade from Hong-Kong is being removed to rejoin the parent division [17th] in Malaya for training in jungle warfare, which will include active participation in the anti-bandit campaign.

'This will enable troops who may have been engaged for many months past on strenuous operations in Malaya to be relieved for rest and training without lessening pressure on the bandits.'

About 2,000 men will be involved in the move. The date is not yet available.

This is the first reduction of British armed strength in Hong-Kong since the 40th Division was formed in the middle of last year, when Chinese Communists were advancing towards South China. The total strength of forces in the colony was then estimated at about 30,000.

The transfer was regarded in Hong-Kong as reflecting: (1) Easing of local tension after the peaceful Communist occupation of the Hong-Kong border; and (2) British determination to subdue the terrorists in Malaya.

It was stated that additional aircraft to support ground troops in Malaya would also be brought to Malaya when the opportunity arose, both by redistribution inside the Far East theatre and by additional aircraft from outside, beginning with the Lincoln squadron from England.

(*Hartlepool Northern Daily Mail*, Tuesday, 14 March 1950)

From September 1949 to the end of June 1950, platoon commander Sub-Lieutenant Nigel Thomas Bagnall of the 1st Battalion, the Green Howards, was engaged in intensive counter-terrorist operations in the Pahang and Negri Sembilan states. Bagnall's – often clandestine – activities proved time and again the value of intelligence gathering in the field that could be converted into successful anti-terrorist operations.

Sub-Lieutenant Bagnall was rewarded with the Military Cross (MC) and subsequently employed in the first six months of 1952 as an intelligence officer. His award appeared in the 1 May 1953 London Gazette. His recommendation citation for the MC, endorsed by Commander-in-Chief Far East Land Forces, General Sir John Harding, reads:

The KGVI Military Cross.

For much of this period he has commanded an isolated detachment at Kampong Menchis [east of Kuala Lumpur]. When he was there in November 1949, the whole area was virtually bandit controlled. In less than two months, he achieved with his force, a measure of success far beyond what could be expected of his small force. The whole area was systematically combed and as a result of Lieutenant Bagnall's personal drive, gallantry and determination, 11 bandit agents were arrested and 16 camps located and destroyed. During the Christmas period, a minor engagement was fought resulting ultimately in the death of one bandit. Lieutenant Bagnall's resolute and untiring devotion to duty resulted in the pacification of the area and to the relief of the Military Forces by the Police.

On 27 May 1950, Lieutenant Bagnall led a patrol, which, acting on information, went by night to a bandit area. With the greatest patience and coolness, he located the bandits and then led a small encircling party through dense jungle behind the bandit camp. After an hour he reached with his patrol an assaulting position 30 yards from a bandit hut. From this bolted three bandits and all three were shot dead by Lieutenant Bagnall and his patrol.

This officer's gallantry, coolness and ruthless energy on operations in the past six months, culminated in this latest success, have become a byword in the Battalion, and have been a source of inspiration to his Platoon and Company and an example, which can seldom have been surpassed.

(National Archives catalogue reference 51 of WO/373/129)

Such was the importance of intelligence sourcing and gathering considered to be, that detailed guidelines were issued to military commanders in the field. Sources were categorised into surrendered CTs, captured CTs, captured documents, killed CTs, informers and the general public, and security force patrols.

Whilst most were deemed of 'obvious value', the identification of a dead CT would be the only method by which the MCP cadre operating in a given area might be established. In the 1958 edition of *Conducting of Anti-terrorist Operations in Malaya*, military commanders were reminded that, 'It must be therefore borne in mind by SF at all times that whilst the killing of [an] individual CT is in itself a worthwhile object, the identification of the body may be of even greater value'.

The importance of body evacuation to the nearest police station was stressed: 'Owing to the speed at which bodies decompose in this climate, ground evacuation will only be used when the carry [by the patrol] is likely to take less than 8 hours'. After this critical period, a helicopter may be called to evacuate the body.

A great emphasis was placed on the taking of photographs of the dead CT. If the patrol did not have a camera, then 'one can be obtained through normal air supplies channels'. Guidelines for 'the successful photography of the body' included:

The face should be washed and the hair brushed.

If 'rigor mortis' has set in, the CT's eyes should be forced open before photographing, to facilitate identification.

A full-face photograph should be taken.

The photograph should be taken at short range.

A minimum of two photographs should be taken.

Fingerprint outfits are issued to all units and full instructions are included in each box. The main principle to be observed is cleanliness, both of the equipment and of the fingers whose prints are being taken.

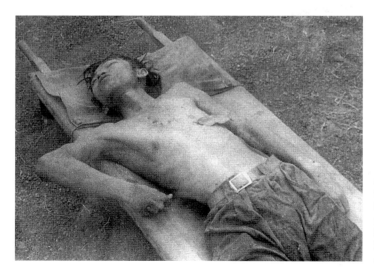

A CT 'kill' awaiting recovery to Special Branch for profiling. (Courtesy Rhodesian African Rifles Regimental Association (UK))

The whole body must be examined ... [for a description of] sex, race, apparent age, height, build and facial features, and teeth, old scars and deformities.

The body must be minutely searched and all documents and other articles by the CT must be recovered.

The handbook highlighted the fact that, 'A great deal of tactical information is provided by SF patrols, whether sent out expressly for that purpose or acquired in the course of other duties'.

For the first six months of 1952, Temporary Captain Nigel Thomas Bagnall's earlier successes in anti-terrorist operations stood him in good stead as intelligence officer and company commander. His personal skills and attributes in jungle operations again proved invaluable, when he was 'employed as Intelligence Officer, but in addition was used for dangerous and difficult operations requiring outstanding skill'.

In July that year, he was appointed company commander, and the following year, he was awarded a Bar to the Military Cross. His award appeared in the 1 May 1953 London Gazette. His recommendation citation for the Distinguished Service Order (DSO), but which was finally

---

GUARDS SERGEANT SAVED HIS COMMANDER IN MALAYA

A Newcastle-on-Tyne sergeant of the Scots Guards has been awarded the Military Medal for heroism during a headquarters patrol battle with terrorists in Malaya last November.

He is Sergt. John McNaught Allan of Blakelaw. His patrol commander, Major Edwyn Inigo Lloyd Mostyn of Horley (Surrey) receives the Military Cross.

The battle started when the patrol heard the sound of chopping and voices 300 yards away. The patrol stalked the noises and, as leading man, Sergt. Allan was the first to spot the enemy when he breasted a small hill. Major Mostyn ran up to him followed by the rest of the patrol – another officer and five men – as soon as fire was opened.

The enemy leader, firing a Bren gun from the hip, led a charge of about half a dozen men, but the Major halted them with a grenade and the action developed into a fight at from five to 20 yards range.

'During the fight,' the citation says, 'Major Mostyn remained standing up under heavy fire at close range. He controlled the fire of his patrol, and working towards the enemy's left flank he caused several casualties by well-aimed grenades.'

The citation indicates that Major Mostyn had been training his men in contact drills during previous months, and 'this small battle went like clockwork and he had no need to issue orders on the spot until the enemy had been routed.'

The citation says of Sergt. Allan that the enemy saw him before the patrol could reach him so he ran forward and opened fire. He remained completely cool throughout, and was to have hit at least two of the enemy with rifle shots.

A bandit who was about to shoot at Major Mostyn from some five yards range was spotted by Sergt. Allan, who shot him in the mouth, thereby probably saving his commander.

(*Yorkshire Post and Leeds Intelligencer*, Wednesday, 3 January 1951)

approved as the Bar to the MC, and endorsed by Commander-in-Chief Far East Land Forces, General Sir Charles Keightley, reads:

On 20 Jan 1952, he led a patrol at night through thick jungle in the GEMAS FOREST RESERVE. At dawn, one terrorist was contacted who threw a grenade at the patrol. Captain Bagnall immediately ran towards him and shot him dead.

On 24 Jan whilst leading a patrol in the jungle of the TAMPIN FOREST RESERVE, Captain Bagnall detected the presence of the enemy. He laid an immediate ambush and in the ensuing action personally killed two terrorists.

On 14 April this officer, whilst on a reconnaissance patrol in the jungle in the TAMPIN area, located a terrorist camp and personally killed a sentry who was later identified as a Branch Committee Member.

On 12 Jun in the TAMPIN area, guided by a surrendered terrorist, Captain Bagnall led a patrol through difficult hilly country to an enemy camp. He attacked the camp and in the engagement four bandits were killed. Captain Bagnall then hunted down and killed the other three terrorists who had tried to break off the engagement, personally killing one of them.

On 14 Aug he located a terrorist track in the jungle in the TAPAH area on which he laid an ambush. Some five hours later three M.R.L.A. [Malayan Races Liberation Army] terrorists entered the ambush and all were killed, one by Captain Bagnall.

On 18 Aug in the TAPAH area he located another track and laid an ambush on it, which resulted in two terrorists being killed and one wounded and captured.

On 29 Sept and 3 Oct, also in the jungle in the TAPAH area, he made contact with small parties of terrorists which resulted in one being killed on each occasion, the second by Captain Bagnall personally. Both were Section Leaders of 39 Ind Platoon M.R.L.A.

This officer's brilliant tactical leadership, his skilful tracking and complete disregard for his personal safety are a byword throughout the Battalion and also, according to surrendered terrorists in the TAMPIN area, amongst the enemy themselves.

His example has been an inspiration to his company and is responsible for maintaining at the highest level their enthusiasm and efficiency right up to the end of their tour of duty in Malaya.

(National Archives catalogue reference 133 of WO/373/131)

Bar to the Military Cross.

6. THE STRUGGLE

The gloomy and misty jungle is dangerously quiet, the faint dripping from last night's rain the only sound. Five metres in front of me the forward scout is frozen in mid-step. He slowly raises his left arm, fist clenched and thumb down, signalling 'bandits near'. We smoothly stop and drop. Muddy green statues melt into the ground. He points downwards in the vague polite way of a Bantu while warily scanning the jungle around him. Cautiously I creep next to him and see the footprints in the composting leaf mould at the side of the track. 'How many, Matias?' I whisper to the hawk-eyed old Nyasa.

> (Second Lieutenant John Essex-Clark, 1st Battalion, Rhodesian African Rifles)

As post-war nationalist fervour resurfaced in many of her colonies and overseas territories, Britain embarked on a difficult and sensitive political programme in which to satisfy the aspirations of self-determination, whilst retaining the loyalty of newly independent nations within the Commonwealth.

Downing Street regarded Malaya of great strategic importance in the defence of that part of the Commonwealth, particularly in terms of a sweeping non-Communist chain of 'friendly' states from the Antipodes to the Indian sub-continent. The loss to the Japanese of the east–west communications pivot in Singapore and the economic-critical resources of Malaya, could not be repeated.

Moscow's global agenda for the expansion of Lenin's Communism and Peking's desire to regionalise Chairman Mao's thoughts did not exclude Southeast Asia. The formation of the Russian-controlled Cominform at Szklarska Poręba in Poland in September 1947, dovetailed with the doctrine of the Soviet Central Committee secretary Andrei Zhdanov, which propounded a world split in two on ideological lines: imperialism, championed by the United States, and the democratic led by the Soviet Union.

Elements of C Squadron, SAS, receive a briefing from commander Major Peter Walls. (Courtesy Jonathan Pittaway)

131 DIED IN MALAYA FIGHTING

Battle casualties in Malaya between May 1, 1948, and February 28, 1950, were 20 officers and 111 other ranks killed and 17 officers and 170 other ranks wounded, said the War Minister, Mr Strachey, in a written reply today.

Two officers and ten other ranks were accidentally killed and one officer and 23 other ranks accidentally wounded.

From January 1, 1948, to December 31, 1949, about 30,000 officers and other ranks (excluding personnel of the Malay Regiment) were admitted to hospital.

In the Far East land forces as a whole, there were in the two years 1948 and 1949, 124 deaths from sickness.

The average rate of British Army troops evacuated through sickness was about 1.1 per cent of the average strength.

(*Gloucestershire Echo*, Wednesday, 19 April 1950)

In striving to collapse the West's capitalist economies by severing the flow of raw materials to the well-established industrial nations, which were dependent on such resources, Moscow's Red Revolution found ready and willing fertile ground in Southeast Asia. For the Soviet Union, it was no difficult task to nurture so-called national liberation movements in Western colonies and dependencies to dislodge their colonial masters from their own countries.

The year 1947 was a watershed for colonial Britain. India and Pakistan fledged, and the sun finally set on the centuries-old British Raj. Moscow fuelled the growth of anti-colonialism in the region with the systematic application of pernicious propaganda, laying total blame at the feet of Britain, France and the Netherlands for running away from the Japanese. In Malaya, the Chinese Communists waged their own battle against the occupying forces, establishing an internal masses-based network of resistance that, with support from Moscow, would be turned on the British administration as soon as the Japanese had been defeated.

To the north, Chiang Kai-shek's Kuomintang – translated as China's National People's Party – was losing its fight to keep China from being overwhelmed by the revolutionary Communist forces of Mao Zedong. In 1949, the Chairman proclaimed the People's Republic of China, profoundly changing the political complexion of Southeast Asia.

The Chinese Communist Party, CCP, was now in a position to offer a tried and tested revolutionary model for other Communist parties in the region to emulate. It came as no surprise, therefore, that the Malayan Communist Party (MCP), with more than 90 per cent of its membership ethnic Chinese, unreservedly opted for Mao's socialist model.

Quickly becoming faithful adherents of Mao's revolutionary techniques, the MCP adopted a strategy of 'armed struggle' in the countryside, while in the cities, subversive elements of the party 'masses' would infiltrate the ranks of the British administration employees. The rural struggle would be inextricably linked with what was happening in the urban centres.

J.P. Morton, former Director of Intelligence during the emergency, described the situation as 'a completely new type of war and that the battle was not just a shooting war by soldiers and police'. In his lecture notes, declassified by the British National Archives in 2007, he states that 'troop enforcements' had increased to the equivalent of two divisions placed in the field in support of the civil administration, which included the police. For Morton, perhaps the 'biggest single mistake' was the administration's negligence of what High Commissioner Templer referred to as the 'battle for the hearts and minds of the people'.

Morton propounded an 'integrated security machine' under a single command. In a hard-hitting indictment of the pre-Templer administration, Morton wrote, 'the Malayan picture could hardly have been blacker'. The murder of High Commissioner Sir Henry Gurney in a CT ambush at Fraser's Hill, north of Kuala Lumpur, on 6 October 1951, saw the Malayan administration 'tottering on the edge of collapse. Control at the top was divided and morale was at rock bottom'. Relations between the police and the army had become increasingly strained and tainted with mutual suspicion.

With the arrival of General Templer, in Morton's words, 'an electric change came over the scene and things literally began to hum'. Templer formed the Director of Operations Committee, over which he had supreme control. The single, combined-operations body comprised the army, civil authorities, police and intelligence. The committee had at its disposal a restructured government propaganda and publicity agency, 'a potent instrument … by which the Government could reach the people and also conduct a psychological offensive to break the morale and discipline of the terrorists'.

Arguably, the only similarity that existed between fighting the imperial Japanese army and the Communist terrorists, was that it took place in the jungles of Southeast Asia. Commander of the Fourteenth Army in the Second World War, General 'Bill' Slim, said of the Nipponese enemy: 'We talk about fighting to the last man and bullet; the Japanese were the only ones who did it.' In sharp contrast, rarely did the Malayan CT dig in and fight. Their tactics comprised hit-and-run strikes and well-concealed surprise ambushes from which escape had been predetermined. Terror was the CT's most effective weapon – the brutal, sadistic maiming and slaughter of defenceless soft targets.

In January 1953, Lieutenant Colonel C.R. Roberts of the Malayan Operational Research Section compiled a memorandum based on patrol and ambush experiences of the emergency up until that date. The dissemination of such analytical dissections of operational reports would greatly assist those in the field tasked with eliminating the CTs.

Roberts's assimilation of historical data revealed the importance of intelligence. Information-based security forces' ambushes and patrols had odds of 1:10 and 1:17 respectively that contact with the enemy would be

British Chief in Malaya Killed in Terrorist Ambush

SIR HENRY GURNEY (53), British High Commissioner in Malaya since 1948, was shot dead by terrorists in an ambush to-day. He was one of Britain's "strong men" in that troubled land.

The Malayan Government issued the following statement: "It is with the deepest regret that we have to announce that His Excellency the High Commissioner, Sir Henry Gurney, was killed in an ambush about 1 o'clock to-day, about two miles below the gap on the Kuala Kubu to Pahang road. Further details will be made available as soon as known."

One of the Europeans in the official party said afterwards that the vehicle carrying the High Commissioner's main police escort broke down near Kuala Kubu, about 25 miles from Fraser's Hill, but Sir Henry's car carried on up the road with a handful of escorting police.

Grim Warfare

Appointed to succeed Sir

SIR HENRY GURNEY

Front cover from the *Northern Daily Mail*, 6 October 1951.

achieved. Conversely, such routine activities where no information was being acted upon, had contact odds of 1:33 and 1:88. On this basis, instructions were issued for military reaction to information received to be given priority.

Addressing the size and formation of security force ambushes, Roberts's exercise showed that 'multiple' as opposed to 'pure linear' (L-shaped, parallel to the enemy's movement) ambushes were 'far more successful'. This was attributed to the fact that additional pre-set ambushes in support of the one initiating the engagement enhanced kill rates, in that the layout provided added opportunities to make contact with any CTs who escaped the first ambush. Roberts did concede, however, that nothing should be set in stone, as the 'linear is potentially effective if bandits walk into it'.

It was Roberts's informed opinion that, wherever the terrain allows it, open-formation patrols should be employed, 'because it is the most effective killing formation and because it is less susceptible to ambush'. Small file-formation patrols with a maximum of fifteen troops, were, according to Roberts, 'most successful in obtaining contacts and in success having made contact'.

Roberts goes on to report that range in an ambush was critical – no more than twenty yards by day and less at night to 'obtain the greatest chance of success'. In the case of patrols, success rates were consistent up to 100 yards, but beyond that range, 'success probably falls off rapidly'.

Based on the number of times fired to achieve a kill, in his memorandum, Roberts proffered a 'respective order of merit of weapons'. For an ambush, the order was Bren light machine gun, M1 or M2 semi-automatic rifles, Owen or Sten sub-machine guns, and rifles. In the case of patrols, the M1 and M2 rifles swapped places with the Bren gun as having the most successful kill to ammunition-expended ratio. Interestingly, Roberts added that there were insufficient cases where shotguns were fired in a contact to 'produce any firm evidence as to its position'.

The time of day or night was also shown to be key in terms of planning. Forty per cent of ambushes were sprung between 7.00 am and 11.00 am, and over 20 per cent between 6.00 pm and 9.00 pm. Roberts found that patrol contacts were relatively uniformly spread during the hours of daylight, with a period from 9.00 am to 1.00 pm producing the greatest number.

Seventy per cent of ambushes were sprung within six hours of setting up, while patrol successes dropped after about six hours of being out on any one day.

Roberts contended that his statistics appear 'to be everything in favour of forcing the bandits to move in small parties', his data showing that the kill rate of CTs was proportionately higher the smaller the group engaged.

Ambushes, at 1:4.7, also enjoyed a considerably greater kill rate than that of patrols, where only 1 in 10 CT contacts resulted in a kill. The ratio of CTs killed to wounded remained 'remarkably constant', at 1 wounded per 1.3 killed in patrol contacts and 1 per 1.2 in ambushes.

Roberts, in concluding his memorandum, stressed the importance of 'steadiness' in both patrols and ambushes. In contacts where strict fire discipline was lacking, ambushes were either sprung without waiting for the maximum number of the enemy to be in the ambush zone, or at too great a distance. Such lack of fire discipline manifested itself in patrols by firing from the hip, resulting in a 'large number of clean misses at 30 yds and under'.

At the time of the declaration of emergency in Malaya in June 1948, the British and Malay security forces had a strength of five British, two Malay and six Gurkha battalions. The Royal Air Force had 100 aircraft based at various stations on the peninsula. The country's police force stood at just over 10,200, comprised almost entirely of ethnic Malays.

BRITAIN' S MARSHALL PLAN QUOTA

Estimates of what Britain can expect to receive in food, raw materials and industrial equipment in the four-and-a-quarter-year period covered by the Marshall Plan, if it is passed in its present form by Congress, are given in a report by the U.S. State Department published today. These are some of the totals:-

Tobacco – £123,250,000 worth
Oil products – 24,000,000 tons
Mining machinery – £18,750,000 worth
Electrical equipment – £35,250,000 worth
Iron and steel – 2,000,000 tons
Timber – £61,250,000 worth
Dried eggs – 100,000 tons

The report forecasts a world food shortage throughout the entire period unless 'very fortunate' crop conditions obtain, and predicts the most serious food position this spring. Serious drought, even for one year, in the U.S. could make it impossible to meet estimates.

For many of her basic foods Britain would continue to rely on other countries – Canada, Argentina and Australia – but in goods of which Britain is now buying none – dried and fresh fruit are typical examples – she would get substantial quantities from the United States.

The report described the Paris Economic Conference's estimates of the meat requirements of Germany and Britain as 'unrealistic', and says that the estimates might have to be revised downwards.

'Dried eggs would be sent to Britain rather than to other countries because the British people are used to them.'

(*Derby Daily Telegraph*, Wednesday, 7 January 1948)

The military was commanded by two Second World War veterans, both with experience of counter-insurgency operations in Greece: Major General Charles Boucher, General Officer Commanding Malayan District, and General Sir Neil Ritchie, Commander-in-Chief, Far East Land Forces (FARELF).

In July, former wartime British officers of Force 136 and Wingate's Chindits, many of whom had since become rubber planters, formed a nation-wide temporary unit to supplement the anti-terrorist operations being conducted by the infantry battalions.

Teams of the Ferret Force – as it was named – went on patrol as light as possible, relying on only the most basic of rations to be parachuted down to them. As a result, the units were highly mobile and difficult to detect by the CTs. Such long-range activities, reminiscent of the Second World War Long Range Desert Group in the North Africa deserts, were necessary to live in the jungle where local inhabitants were befriended to assist with intelligence gathering.

Ambush! (Courtesy Rhodesian African Rifles Regimental Association (UK))

Commanded by the highly decorated Burma veteran, Lieutenant Walter Walker, the Ferret Force was, however, met with disfavour by both the army and the police, who had a dislike for 'private armies'. In November, the unit was disbanded.

A few years later, the legacy of the Ferret Force would inspire Special Air Service (SAS) deep-penetration operations into the Malayan jungles.

The arrival in Malaya of Lieutenant General Sir Harold Briggs as Director of Operations, and High Commissioner Sir Henry Gurney, saw a redefining of the manner in which anti-terrorist operations were being executed – CTs and the local populace had to be kept apart permanently.

Following the assassination of Gurney in a CT ambush on 6 October 1951, British prime minister Winston Churchill sent large numbers of additional troops to Malaya. General Sir Gerald Templer took over as high commissioner in Kuala Lumpur in early 1952. Commander-in-Chief Far East, General Sir John Harding then called on the unorthodox Major ' Mad' Mike Calvert, who had become renowned for his unconventional – and often questionable – special operations in the Burmese jungles of the Second World War.

After six months of 'going jungle' and blending in with locals, Calvert officially recommended that a special force be raised specifically to undertake deep-jungle operations to eradicate CTs, their camps and their food sources. His recommendations were adopted, and Calvert formed an SAS-styled unit: the Malayan Scouts (Special Air Service Regiment).

Initially, recruitment was restricted to the region, but this only attracted 100 men, titled 'A' Squadron. A reservist pool of former members of the wartime 'M' Squadron of 21SAS provided a second source of recruits, this time from Britain. Redesignated 'B' Squadron, Malayan Scouts, the new arrivals were shocked by the unruly, heavy drinking, bearded Malayan Scouts they met up with.

Calvert then went to Southern Rhodesia, from where Colonel David Sterling, who had founded the original SAS in 1941, had suggested to the British War Office that 'the Rhodesians would be better utilised as parachute-trained troops specialising in deep penetration operations against CTs in the jungles of Malaya'. In Salisbury, 120 suitable candidates were selected as the Southern Rhodesia Far East Volunteer Unit (SRFEVU), redesignated 'C' Squadron on arrival in Malaya. Finally, a fourth squadron, comprising territorials of the 21SAS (Artists' Rifles) arrived in Malaya, where they became 'D' Squadron. The unit was now retitled 22SAS Regiment. A New Zealand Squadron joined in 1955.

The first base was at Dusun Tua, just east of Kuala Lumpur, described by Trooper Geoff Turner-Dauncey of C Squadron as an 'overgrown camp that looked as if it had been a hot springs pleasure resort abandoned due to terrorist action'. Proficiency in the use of small arms

"MAD MIKE" CALVERT HOME FROM BURMA

The scene is a jungle clearing well behind the Jap lines in Burma. Rations are being issued to a weary, bedraggled bunch of Chindit raiders who have been paralysing Jap supply lines for weeks.

The rations – a handful of rice per man – have been the same for ten days. A little Cockney orderly gets his, gazes solemnly at the small white pile in his hand for a moment and then murmurs, "Blimey, turned out rice again!"

"And that," said 31-year-old Brigadier James Michael Calvert, D.S.O. and Bar, United States Silver Star, to me, "helps to explain why the British soldier is good enough to knock hell out of the yellow men wherever they meet."

It was easy to get Brigadier Calvert – the almost legendary "Mad Mike" – to talk about the men who fought with him at Mogaung, who accompanied him on brilliantly daring demolition raids behind enemy lines in Burma.

Not so easy to get this stocky, broad-shouldered, barrel-chested, clear-eyed former Army welterweight champion to talk about the exploits that have made him one of the most colourful figures of the whole Burma campaign to date.

"Mad Mike" was a brigadier at 30. First saw the Japanese fighting man in action against the Chinese in 1937, when, he says, "I had a grandstand view from pillboxes and learned quite a lot."

Helped to lug cases of dynamite incredible distances to blow up Japanese communications; charged with rifle and bayonet along with his men of the 77th Infantry Brigade in battles that led up to the all-important capture of Mogaung, our real turning point in Burma.

(*Daily Herald*, Monday, 22 January 1945)

was practised over and over, as quick reflexes at short range was far more critical in the jungle confines compared to firing over long ranges.

Relatively little time was spent on tracking, as, apart from the fact that CTs generally wore smooth-soled footwear, any footprint found in the jungle had to be treated with suspicion.

Demolition training mainly proved of benefit when clearing aerial drop zones and landing zones for helicopters, using plastic explosives and Cordtex detonating cord.

Describing the *ulu* – Malayan jungle – as 'no walk in the park', Turner-Dauncey elaborates:

> From the moment you step into the *ulu* that familiar fetid rank odour unique to the jungle immediately encompasses you, and the humidity hits you as you become conscious of that dank surreal atmosphere. In no time at all you are soaked from perspiration and from the wet undergrowth; the warm heavy monsoon rain also adds its daily share of moisture. Unless you follow an elephant trail, rocky riverbed, or some other clear path, you have to hack your way through dense undergrowth. This is not only exhausting, requiring constant change-around of personnel doing the hacking, but cannot be done silently. The main disadvantage in choosing an open trail is that you leave yourself open to ambush.
>
> At times it is necessary to cross mountain ranges on foot. This becomes an exhausting exercise when carrying heavy packs, and slipping and sliding as you try to gain secure footholds on the steep and muddy slopes. Despite the exhaustion, constant vigilance

Jungle patrol. (Courtesy Rhodesian African Rifles Regimental Association (UK))

THE RHODESIA HERALD, FRIDAY, MARCH 16, 1951

En Route For Malaya

Members of the Rhodesian Far East Unit on their way to Durban, where they embarked on Wednesday night for Malaya. The men found letter-writing a popular way of passing the time on the train-journey. They are (left to right) Ptes. A. W. Strong, R. Alexander, W. J. van Heerden and T. E. Chappell.

Members of the future C Squadron SAS, start their journey to Malaya. (Courtesy Jonathan Pittaway)

must be maintained as there is the danger that when CTs set up defensive positions on high ground, the exhausted leading troop can walk into them unawares.

Some of the most gruelling terrains the troops had to cope with were in mangrove swamps, where it is difficult to find your bearings. As you slip and slide on the roots, you can easily miss a foothold and suddenly find yourself up to the neck in muddy water. It is difficult enough for an individual to traverse a swamp in daylight.

At times you walk in deep shade a canopy formed by giant trees. Because the sun is blotted out, the undergrowth is sparse enough to walk normally, where your footsteps cannot be heard as you walk on the thick layers of rotting vegetation. In fact, the jungle is very quiet during the day where the odd snake slithers across your path, and evidence of the diggings of wild pig and tracks of other animals can be seen.

From the moment we stepped into the jungle until we returned to base we got soaked, and stayed wet. In that humidity, one has to learn to cope with impetigo skin disease including ringworm, leeches and other ailments. Insect and leech bites soon began to fester, and ringworm, many forms of eczema, and athlete's foot resulted in widespread ulceration of the skin. Ointments only aggravated rotting flesh, so where possible penicillin wound powder was applied to open sores.

With our operational dress torn and rotting, and stinking of sweat, rifle oil and decaying vegetation, it was common practice to burn our clothes on returning to base. For a while troops returning to base from operations looked rather like clowns: wearing just PT shorts, sandals and berets, their bodies lavishly painted with mercurochrome, gentian violet and Whitfield's Lotion until their skin problems healed.

The indigenous Sakai and Dyak trackers from the Iban tribe in Borneo were totally at home in the jungle. But in no way can it be considered as the long-term habitat of the European serviceman.

Radio communications in the jungle were key, but often unreliable. (Courtesy Jonathan Pittaway)

A VC SEEKS ADVENTURE

Private Bill Speakman, the Korean VC, was demobilised yesterday after almost eight years, Army service but his sojourn in civilian life is to be temporary. He announced that he is to seek fresh fields of excitement with the Special Air Service fighting terrorists in Malaya.

"I believe," he said, "that by volunteering I shall be accepted much sooner than if I remained in the Army and sought a transfer through the usual channels. It will be more interesting and exciting abroad than serving at home. Anyhow, I like the Far East and the life."

Yesterday he received from Major T.G. Coverdale, Commanding Officer of The King's Own Scottish Borderers Depot at Berwick, the Victoria Cross which Private Speakman had left at the Depot for safe custody.

Private Speakman expects to go within a week or two to the London HQ of the Special Air Service whose training is done at Singapore, to discuss his enlistment.

[In spite of being wounded in the leg and shoulder, Speakman charged the attacking Chinese fifteen times to allow his company, many of whom were wounded, to withdraw from United Hill, Korea, on 4 November 1951. Upon running out of grenades, according to the press, Speakman started to throw beer bottles at the enemy, giving rise to his Victoria Cross being referred to as 'the beer bottle VC'. This would be the first Victoria Cross presented by Queen Elizabeth II.]

(*Yorkshire Post and Leeds Intelligencer*, Friday, 20 February 1953)

Members of C Squadron SAS on their arrival in Singapore prior to being deployed into Malaya. (Courtesy Craig Fourie)

Lieutenant Colonel Ronald Francis Reid-Daly CLM, DMM, MBE (Rtd), commander of the Rhodesian special forces unit, the Selous Scouts, during that country's counter-insurgency war of the 1970s, was a C Squadron SAS volunteer in 1951. Reid-Daly, then a sergeant, recalls one particular patrol during his two-year tour of duty in Malaya. He not only provides a detailed insight into a typical patrol during the emergency, but reveals how the bond amongst brothers-in-arms was strengthened through tragedy:

We had been dropped by vehicle at a particular point on the main tar road and were moving along a ridge line when the incident happened. This was to be a six-week operation and the modus operandi was as follows: the Squadron, comprising about ninety men, would move in single file through the jungle – it was the only way you could move. The leading troop was responsible for map-reading and at the conclusion of that day's march it would move to the rear for the following day. However, every man in the Squadron map-read and at the hourly halts each troop would confer and decide on its position. Troop commanders would then move to Squadron Headquarters Troop and a similar conference would take place with Major Walls who was an excellent map-reader [Major Peter Walls went on to command the Rhodesian army in the 1970s, with the rank of lieutenant general]. Sometimes there would be some ferocious argument in venomous whispers (you never spoke in normal tones) but generally there was consensus. Headquarters Troop always travelled behind the leading troop which changed every day.

Each man commenced operations with a seventy-pound pack and on top of each pack, a radio battery, which weighed exactly nine pounds, was added. There were no section radios, only a 68 Set for each troop which, in conventional units, was based at Brigade and Battalion Headquarters. The set, without a battery, weighed twenty-eight pounds, and only Morse code was used. We carried seven days' rations but these had to last ten days, and on the eleventh day, weather permitting, we would get another seven days' rations in an airdrop.

I think it was about 3pm on that particular day that the shooting started. We always tried to move along ridge lines, as nine times out of ten there was a game track running along it which made the going much easier. This particular track was used by elephants. We discovered after the incident that it was also used by the CTs who used to step into the elephant footprints which were full of water, thus disguising their own.

On this particular day, Vic Visagie was the leading scout for the lead troop, I think it was 13 Troop. I was the Troop Sergeant of 11 Troop and we were at the end [of the line formation]. When the firing broke out I quickly moved up the line to find out what was going on. We had no troop radio to communicate with each other quickly. The 68 Set would have to be unpacked, an aerial thrown up into the trees and the radio frequency tuned in, all of which took a great deal of time.

When I got to the head of the column I saw Sergeant 'Tickey' McLoughlin lying behind a log. I still have a vivid picture of his red beard. I asked him what had happened and he pointed to a body lying in front of him – it was Vic Visagie, who had collected a burst of three rounds in the face from a Sten gun. The shooter was the [CT] camp sentry and he was positioned just off the track. Vic was shot from about ten yards away. The leading troop had pushed ahead and had located a recently vacated camp just off the track. The occupants, some twelve in number, had been eating and had scattered when the firing broke out, leaving their unfinished meal of tinned fish and rice behind.

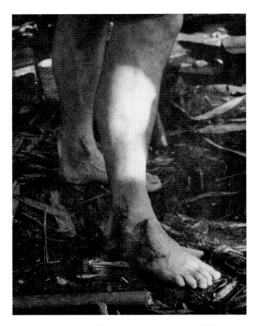

Leeches, curse of the wet jungles of Malaya.
(Courtesy Jonathan Pittaway)

I spoke to Major Walls who asked me to bury Vic. Men of 11 Troop then started digging a grave while I plotted and marked the position on the map. I then helped with the digging using my panga. While I was busy doing this, a new member of my troop (Pretorius) who had recently arrived with a bunch of reinforcements from Rhodesia said, 'Sarge, why don't you get some embalming material dropped in and I'll embalm him. We can carry him out to the road and it will save us having to come back at a later stage to dig him up.'

I sat back on my heels and said, 'What do you know about embalming?' 'Oh,' says Pretorius, 'I'm an undertaker in Civvy Street.'

I shot across to Major Walls who thought it a great idea. To cut a long story short, a light aircraft flew over, made contact, and dropped a package with a long coloured streamer attached to it. Luckily, it landed right in the centre of us. Pretorius asked me to assist him embalm Vic, but when he described the procedures, I hastily declined his request. Pretorius went ahead on his own.

A litter was made and the following morning Lance Corporal Campling took off towards the road with a small patrol including Private Frank Wentzel and an enormous cloud of flies. Vic was buried with full military honours in the military cemetery in Kuala Lumpur.

Both Lieutenant General Peter Walls and Lieutenant Colonel Ron Reid-Daly passed away in 2010.

Brigadier John 'Digger' Essex-Clark, DSM (retd) served in the Rhodesian army before joining the Australian army in 1963. He has served with the Australian, British, United States and Rhodesian armies, and, in the course of his military career, has commanded in action troops from Malaya, South Africa, Rhodesia, Vietnam, Britain, New Zealand, the United States and Australia.

Forever outspoken, the retired Brigadier Essex-Clark, who now lives in Canberra, Australia, remains critical of 'army obsession with technology and the paucity of subtle tactical thinking'. Essex-Clark still maintains an absolute faith in the capabilities of the infantryman in combat, but bemoans, in his critical opinion, the lack of strong, competent leadership in modern armies which he views as having a 'surfeit of military dilettantes and budding bureaucrats and a dearth of warrior-chiefs'. He singles out the 'pussyfooters' in Vietnam and the 'bastardisation' of the Australian military academy at Duntroon.

In Malaya, the then Second Lieutenant Essex-Clark would realise a vast experience of anti-terrorist operations, from which he analytically developed his personal theories on counter-insurgency.

Commander of C Squadron, Major Peter Walls, standing with crossed kukris held over his head, poses with Ghurkhas. (Courtesy Jonathan Pittaway)

The RAF Scottish Aviation Pioneer was used extensively in Malaya for tasks such as casualty evacuation. The versatile aircraft was able to operate out of very short, rudimentary airstrips, requiring as little as 225 ft in which to take off. (Courtesy Rhodesian African Rifles Regimental Association (UK))

AUSTRALIAN FORCES MAY GO TO MALAYA

But British Units May Be Reduced

The possibility of Australian and New Zealand Forces being sent to Malaya is likely to be discussed during the Commonwealth Prime Ministers' Conference which opens in London a week next Monday.

Both the Australian and New Zealand Governments are believed to be willing to station small ground or air forces in Malaya, but no final decision is expected until after the SEATO [The Southeast Asia Treaty Organization, for collective defence in the region] Conference in Bangkok next month.

With the SEATO meeting in mind, the Prime Ministers will not consider the defence of Malaya in isolation, but will try to work out an agreed Commonwealth approach to the whole problem of South-East Asia defence as it is likely to arise at Bangkok.

The Prime Ministers are likely to hold their defence talks independently of their main plenary sessions in order not to offend Mr Nehru's [India's first prime minister] susceptibilities. Mr Nehru is anxious to use the London Conference as a platform for his neutralist approach, and he will find any mention of SEATO an embarrassment.

The question of the sending of Australian and New Zealand troops to Malaya has in recent months been actively studied both in Canberra and Wellington. Neither Government has given any firm indication as to the Forces it might make available, but there have been reports of the Australians being willing to spare an infantry battalion and of the New Zealanders contributing a fighter squadron (there is one stationed in Cyprus).

At present the defence of Malaya is being carried out entirely by British, Gurkha and Colonial forces, and one of the arguments previously advanced in favour of Australian and New Zealand participation was that it would enable some British Forces to be brought home.

This, however, was before the Communist threat in Indo-China crystallised, and before the setting-up of SEATO. Now, any Australian and New Zealand Forces sent to Malaya will be only partly concerned with the defence of the peninsula. Their other, and primary, function would be to form part of the SEATO 'fire brigade' force.

(Yorkshire Post and Leeds Intelligencer, Thursday, 20 January 1955)

Following in the path of the deployment in Malaya in March 1951 of 100 Rhodesians, known as the South East Asia Volunteer Unit (SEAVU) and subsequently C Squadron 22SAS (Malayan Scouts), in February 1956, the first elements of the 1st Battalion, Rhodesian African Rifles (RhAR) disembarked at Singapore. From here, they moved up to Kluang in Johore to join their sister battalion, the 1st Northern Rhodesia Regiment (NRR), whom they were due to relieve.

The training team spent about three weeks in the jungle with the NRR, after which they moved to Batu Bahat to join the 1st Fiji Infantry Regiment (1FIR), who were veteran jungle fighters. The men from both units got on extremely well together.

Brigadier John
'Digger' Essex-Clark
DSM (Australia)
at the National
Memorial
Arboretum in
England in July 2015.
(Photo Gerry van
Tonder)

After eight years of anti-terrorist operations in the peninsula, the CT concentrations had been broken up into small groups, subverting the rural populace in order to gain supplies and recruits. The task of the security forces was to prevent the CTs from regrouping by destroying base camps and food caches.

While the advance party was being jungle-trained, the rest of 1RhAR disembarked from HMT *Empire Clyde* at Singapore in April 1956. They immediately moved out to the Far East Land Forces (FARELF) training centre – Nyasa Camp – in Johore, thirty-two miles north-east of Singapore. Here, the battalion formed part of 99 Gurkha Infantry Brigade, 17th Gurkha Division.

Intense jungle training ensued over the following weeks. At Kota Tinggi, short marches were made into the tall, thick *belukar* – secondary jungle – so as to experience the local conditions that were dominated by Malayan rainstorms. So-called jungle-lane range shooting practice was conducted frequently.

The battalion's area of operations was to be south of Segamat in the Cha'ah, Labis and Bekok areas. Headquarters was set up Cha'ah, 100 miles north of Singapore. Commanding 8 Platoon, C Company, was Second Lieutenant Essex-Clark. The platoon comprised thirty-two askaris in three rifle sections. Together with Platoon Warrant Officer Pisayi Muzerecho and the platoon NCOs (non-commissioned officers), Essex-Clark had spent seventeen months training the men from raw recruits. In his autobiography, *Maverick Soldier*, Essex-Clark

Officers of the 1st Battalion, the Rhodesian African Rifles Malaya contingent. Essex-Clark is standing in the back row, fifth from the left. (Courtesy Rhodesian African Rifles Regimental Association (UK))

describes his relationship with his men as 'very close, in fact, paternal as I was both their teacher and their leader'.

During his two years in Malaya, when on patrol, Essex-Clark had three rifle sections in his platoon, each of about seven men. He patrolled with a scout ahead, usually armed with a shotgun, and accompanied by a reaction group of three men. Next came the section's main firepower – the Bren gunner – and an NCO armed with a Patchett (Sterling) 9mm sub-machine gun. The Bren had a 28-round magazine with every third round a tracer.

The sections operated from a platoon base, the headquarters of the platoon commander assisted by a warrant officer and a sergeant, as well as a radio operator, a medic and the platoon commander's batman.

Essex-Clark's combat patrols moved in single file with five yards between each soldier. He writes:

> When my platoon patrolled, I travelled not less than ten metres behind the scout, with the corporal of the leading section immediately in front of me. When navigation was difficult I would be close behind the scout. Pisayi moved behind the lead section ready to take over if I became a casualty. He had the radio operator and the medic with him. Sergeant Gondocondo [sic] travelled in the rear. A well-trained African platoon moved very fluidly and fast in jungle compared with the British platoons ... The askari could track well ... I had very good fighting NCOs and Pisayi and Gondocondo were magnificent. I was confident that my men were fit, well-trained and motivated. We had no reason to fail in action.

By May 1956, 1RhAR had experienced small successes, and had become well-practised in airdrops, ambush and transport drills. The troops began to take part in operations, discovering that the search for CTs would be compounded by the presence of rubber poachers, and that radio communications in the *ulu* – jungle – were unsatisfactory.

On 1 June, RhAR officers from the first draft went down to Singapore to bid farewell to the Fiji Infantry Regiment, which had been their mentor prior to the arrival of the rest of the

MINISTERS HOPEFUL OF MALAYA

Mr James Griffiths, Colonial Secretary, and Mr John Strachey, War Secretary, both assured the House of Commons last night that steps are being taken to end the emergency in Malaya. A plan had been prepared and was being put into operation by the Forces under Gen. Briggs.

'I must warn the House not to expect swift and spectacular results,' said Mr Griffiths. Having seen the difficulties of terrain and communications, I do not under-estimate the task. But I know it a task we can face squarely and confidently.

'The vast majority of people in Malaya of every community are opposed to the Communists.'

Mr Strachey said substantial reinforcements of land and air forces were arriving in Malaya. Mr Strachey, who with Mr Griffiths recently returned from a visit to the troops in Malaya and Hong-kong, said he found all units of the British Army showing a most determined spirit.

'British troops serving in Malaya, their relatives, and the nation as a whole may rest assured that we are in no sense attempting to stop a national movement of the Malayan people seeking independence. On the contrary, we are aiding the great majority of the people of Malaya in preventing a small, but well organised, minority from seizing power in their country.'

Mr L.D. Gammans (Con. Hornsey) spoke of the danger of allowing the new Government in China [under Chairman Mao Zedong] to open consulates in Malaya and asked if we were getting co-operation from Siam as regards infiltration generally.

Mr Griffiths replied: 'There is very good co-operation between the authorities in Siam and ourselves on movement across the frontier.'

Speaking of squatters, Mr Griffiths said it would be a mistake to think that all of them [predominantly ethnic Chinese] were enemies.

(*Western Morning News*, Thursday, 22 June 1950)

battalion. That evening, the first operational order from 63 Brigade arrived, informing them that they were to take part in Operation Huckster.

The RhAR's role would be to give the impression that they were holding a training exercise in the Jemaluang–Mersing area. Then, under cover of darkness, they would be moved out and deployed along the Jemaluang–Kluang road. Together with other British units, companies of troops, once dropped off, disappeared into the dark jungle, sealing off an area which had not seen a military presence for some time. All units would then work their way from the cordon perimeter towards the centre of the ring-fenced zone, with the objective of flushing out any CTs, who would then be pushed into the field of fire of another and eliminated.

At first light on 5 June, the companies began heading towards the Kahang River, the first cordon boundary. That evening, information was received that, an hour earlier, twenty to thirty well-armed CTs had raided Kahang village, eight miles north-east of the RhAR's eastern boundary. The guerrillas had taken a large stock of food, for which they had – unusually – paid

HMT *Empire Clyde* arrived in Singapore with 1RhAR in April 1956. (Courtesy Brigadier John 'Digger' Essex-Clark)

A patrol makes its way through a flooded watercourse. (Courtesy Rhodesian African Rifles Regimental Association (UK))

$130. Brigade was immediately notified and a follow-up mounted by elements from the South Wales Borderers and 5 Malay Regiment. At the same time, an order went out to halt the RhAR, and for them to face north-east and deploy into killer stop groups, ambushing all approaches from that direction. Communications, however, were so bad that the RhAR companies were still patrolling southwards by first light the following morning.

Fortuitously, an RAF Auster found the RhAR's C Company and dropped a message informing their commander, Major Godwin, of the change of plan. All but one of the company platoons were contacted and redeployed accordingly.

The day of 7 June was spent patrolling and laying ambushes. The next day, 2 Platoon reported finding a fresh CT resting place, from where the troops followed tracks for some 700 yards before they were lost. The platoon was ordered to remain where it was.

Meanwhile, the drive by 5 Malay Regiment failed to deliver, or in army parlance, had produced a 'lemon'. Major Salt's B Company was ordered to sweep the valley to their north-east, which the CTs had been using used as a hideout after raids on local villages and plantations. By this time, RAF 19 Flight Liaison Austers had been brought in to relay and maintain ground communications.

After a ration-replenishment airdrop that Sunday, the RhAR's B Company was ordered to change from the north-easterly direction they had been moving in the previous four days, and head south towards the river. The South Wales Borderers had two kills and a capture in the Niyor area, so it seemed a little odd sending the RhAR away when CTs were known to be in the area.

By 14 June, all RhAR platoons were at designated points along the Kahang River, where patrols found nothing put small patches of sweet potatoes. The next day, an air strike was called in on a suspected CT base camp, but the only casualty was an RhAR NCO who had burned his foot with a marker balloon.

The basics: a security force camp in the jungle. (Courtesy Rhodesian African Rifles Regimental Association (UK))

On 20 June, one of Major McCullagh's D Company patrols fired on a khaki-clad figure moving along an embankment. The presumed CT, however, escaped unharmed. Pursuing his tracks, the patrol then came across several wild-pig traps, one of which contained a pig, thus revealing the fugitive's occupation. The patrol ate the pig.

All companies were back at base camp by the end of June, the operation having lasted for twenty-six days of tiring foot-slogging without any sign of the enemy. Operation Huckster, in fact, was so typical of operations in Malaya.

RhAR companies continued to conduct regular patrols and ambushes from their base camps. There would be more than one occasion where trigger-finger-ready soldiers came close to killing civilians, including local Home Guard members, who were innocently attending to their daily chores in the jungle, seemingly oblivious to the life-threatening dangers found in a war zone. Jungle patrolling in Malaya was indeed fraught with difficulties, not least among them the delicate task of distinguishing friend from foe.

The QUEEN has been graciously pleased to give orders for the following promotions in, and appointments to, the Most Excellent Order of the British Empire, in recognition of distinguished service in Malaya for the period 31st August to 31st December, 1957:

To be Additional Members of the Military Division of the said Most Excellent Order:

Major Christopher Bernard McCULLAGH

Recommendation citation as endorsed by General Sir Francis Festing, Commander-in-Chief, Far East Land Forces:

Since April 1956 Major McCULLAGH has displayed a standard of devotion to duty, personal courage, determination and zeal far in excess of that demanded in the normal course of duty. His skill in operations coupled with his boundless energy and determination to seek out and kill the enemy have been a byword throughout the Battalion. This officer's personal contribution to the Unit's effort against the enemy has been outstanding, and without question has been a most significant factor in achieving the successes so arduously secured.

His personal leadership and constant concern and endeavours on behalf of his men has been most marked throughout his long period in the jungle.

He has set an example of devotion to duty of the highest order and has richly earned the superb reputation he now enjoys within the unit as a company commander of outstanding merit.

He has been recently appointed Second-in-Command of the Battalion. His zeal, his cheerful unbounded enthusiasm together with his flare [sic] for sound administration has been thrown whole-heartedly into his new job. The extremely high standard of maintenance and morale within the regiment is very largely due to Major McCullagh's unfailing devotion to unselfish duty.

This officer's service in Malaya has been of such a high quality that it richly deserves recognition of a very high order.

(*London Gazette*, 23 May 1958 and WO/373/135)

A marker balloon, its base filled with lithium hydride and water to produce hydrogen, was used to direct helicopters to a pre-cleared landing zone, or LZ. (Courtesy Brigadier John 'Digger' Essex-Clark)

In October that year, the battalion was operating in the Tangkak Jemantah area in Johore. At this time, C Company had its first contact with CTs, when an askari on the flank of an ambush heard sounds to the rear. As he spun around, he saw a man in khaki barely ten yards from him. As the CT fled, the askari fired two quick shots. The CT was seen to stagger with the second shot, but he escaped without any sign.

RhAR's A and B companies were back in the Bekok area by the end of October. C and D companies were deployed into the Palong area, where the Muar River was so swollen from persistent heavy rain, that collapsible boats had to be employed to effect a crossing. Introducing much-needed humour into the situation, one of the men wrote in his diary: 'The Muar Regatta is now on and the battalion produced some very fine oarsmen'.

The action-starved RhAR battalion, desperate for a contact in which to test their training, ambushed the rail line at Bekok on seven successive nights. Everyone in camp took turns at

Order of the British Empire (Military).

leading the patrols –intelligence officer, assistant adjutant, medical officer, regimental sergeant major, quartermaster, ration sergeant, regimental signals officer, education sergeant, pay sergeant, intelligence sergeant, orderly room warrant officer and headquarters' company sergeant major. It was, however, all in vain.

Information was then received from The Royal Lincolnshires in the Bahau that they had had a fleeting engagement with Hor Lung's 32 Independent Platoon, which was heading towards the Palong River. A and B companies, RhAR, were immediately moved from the Bekok area to take up positions alongside C and D companies in anticipation of finally making contact with an enemy hitherto known only as a name of pieces of paper and maps.

On 9 November, a half-section from Second Lieutenant de Bruyn's 7 Platoon saw sixteen pack-laden CTs moving east. Section Commander Corporal Munyameni, not holding out for commands, launched an immediate attack. Caught unawares, the CTs bombshelled in all directions. One CT, trying to appear invisible behind the bole of a tree was shot and killed

Early that same morning, C Company's 8 Platoon, commanded by the newly promoted – and acting company commander – Lieutenant Essex-Clark, was patrolling back towards company headquarters. He had split his platoon into three-man sections to cover more ground. A platoon corporal led his half-section to the west, leaving while Essex-Clark with a rifleman and the Bren gunner, headed south-east.

The officer led his two men across a deep swampy creek, or *sungai*, before coming to a halt, straining their ears for any indication of human presence. Essex-Clark continues:

A weird feeling often alerts me to a threat before sight or sound reaches me. I spin around to the east, diving to the ground, Patchett ready, before the crackling 9mm fire and the rhythmic thump-thump-thump thump-thump of a Bren echoes through the jungle, blending with the crump of shot guns and faint shouts. I had just been thinking that Hor Lung had got away so I hope our patrols have not run into one another. Then with the distinctive 'crang' of grenades, which we do not carry, I know that we have a contact with terrorists. We melt into a three-man ambush on the ridge and wait.

Forty metres away, in a densely foliaged creek, we hear a group bashing its way downstream. We catch glimpses of their khaki uniforms: CTs! They are moving fast

River travel by indigenous dugout canoe. (Courtesy Rhodesian African Rifles Regimental Association (UK))

towards the Palong and are now past our patrols. I crab-scuttle down the flat ridge behind us and hear Mabgwe and Zacha [his men] following me. We'll cut them off and attempt to engage them closer at the point where the creek wends its way close to the northern spur of our ridge.

We reach the swampy creek at the same time as the CTs are scurrying by. They're on the far bank and not easy to see clearly but there seem to be about six of them armed with rifles and Sten guns. They're chirruping and urging each other on in Chinese. Fair odds. We three have the initiative. They have not shot at us; therefore they have not seen us. We run, crouched, and crawl closer to find better firing positions. They see us first and fire wildly. We fire back and charge in. I shoot at two CTs 25 metres in front of me. One is firing at me; he stumbles; I fire and bowl him over, but I can't see my lads with me.

Bullets thump into trees near me. I feel alone but keep scrambling forward. I fire my 'signature', a one three double tap, twice, to let the others know where I am. Thunk. My Patchett jams! I mutter. I change magazines. Still jammed. I can hear firing on my left: Mabgwe. 'Get up with me you dingwit!' I mutter. I look in the ejection opening. It is plugged with moss and crud. I drop into the *lopak* [pool or puddle] swamp behind a log and quickly clear out the mess with my finger. It burns. I see blood mixed in the water. Not mine. I've lost my jungle hat and feel awkward and exposed without it. I bind my head with my sweat rag

---

MALAYAN H.G. IN ACTION

Operation Launched Against Jungle Terrorists

Malayan Home Guards have launched their own operation against Communist Terrorists without the aid of Commonwealth forces, for the first time since the anti-Communist emergency began almost eight years ago, reports Reuter.

The Home Guards, mostly Malays, have already shot dead one Communist Terrorist near Dungung, East Malaya, since they have been mobilized for full-time duty.

Home Guard service is compulsory in all villages and towns in 'black' (Communist threatened) parts of Malaya. Elsewhere, volunteers have joined for up to six months. They receive seven shillings sterling a day.

In Selangor, Home Guard sections have been integrated into platoons of the First Battalion, the Royal Hampshire Regiment, with 'excellent results', according to Lieut.-General Sir Geoffrey Bourne, the director of operations.

Young Hampshire N.C.O.'s have instructed the Home Guard in jungle warfare and the use of automatic shotguns. The mixed patrols live and fight together and commands are given in a mixture of Malay and English.

(*Hartlepool Northern Daily Mail*, Friday, 6 April 1956)

---

and roll forward over the log. A spray of bullets showers me with muck. They must know that there are only three of us.

I scramble sideways and crawl through the swamp, noticing, of all things, dozens of pitcher plants which trap insects. I stand in a tree buttress and fire a burst in the direction of the CTs. I hear Zachariah shout and the thump-thump, thump-thump double-tap of his Bren on my right.

We keep stumbling and scrambling up the incline getting even further behind them. We cannot keep up and we are the ones firing wildly now. They fire back at us with controlled bursts. I can't see them but there now seem to be many more than six. Their bullets crack overhead. I see blood splattered on a log. 'Steady, buster,' I caution myself. 'You're supposed to be commanding a company, not two men.'

I shout, 'Stop!' The CTs have gone over the ridge line ahead. I give them a short final burst for luck and bravado and put on my last full magazine.

Zachariah joins me. We are both excited, grinning and panting. He has only one magazine left. We find Mabgwe. He's a little shaky and has a badly sprained ankle. Supporting him, we move warily back to the patrol base.

Everyone in the base is euphoric. Our patrols return. We send out search parties for the wounded and the dead. I radio back to headquarters to tell them that we've had a successful contact and will confirm later the details of CTs killed or suspected wounded. I also asked for tracker-dog teams to help us follow-up. It is the battalion's first success, for which we'd trained and waited nearly two years.

I cool down and squat, exhausted, against a tree buttress, next to my radio operator. The body of the dead CT lies next to me on a makeshift stretcher of cut saplings, poncho and nylon cord.

The dead CT was later identified as Chim Ah Li, the deputy section leader of their platoon. Four packs, a Sten gun and four magazines were recovered.

Early in February 1957, the RhAR's B Company returned to their Labis Camp in preparation for food-denial operations around Labis, Chaah and Bekok. This entailed increased patrolling along the boundaries between jungle and rubber plantations, and in doing so, denying CTs access to local village sympathisers from whom they would source essential food supplies.

At that time, Lieutenant Bob Graver, a policeman from Kampong Aur, reported that, while patrolling south from Kampong Kong King on the Sekin River, he had had a fleeting contact with a lone armed CT. The guerrilla escaped, but his very presence in the area led the authorities to conclude that it was realistic to assume that CTs, around sixty miles to the north, could transport supplies to their desperate comrades in the food-denial areas around Cobble.

As a consequence, on 21 February 1957, the RhAR's 4 Platoon, commanded by Lieutenant David Heppenstall, and accompanied by Graver, was airlifted from Segamat to Kampong Aur seventy miles away, from where they made their way downstream to Kampong Kong King by sampan – a distance of thirty miles.

Heppenstall regularly sent his sections out on prolonged jungle patrols, but during their six-week stay, only one CT was killed. The enemy was frustratingly elusive, a situation

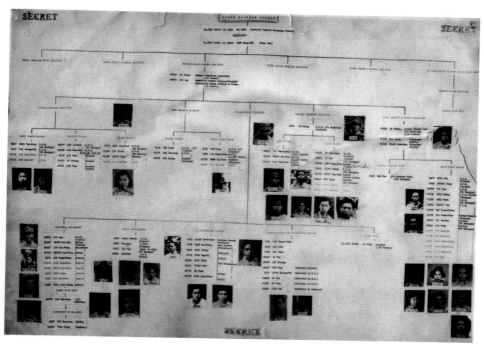

Military structure of the Southern Malaya Bureau of the Malayan Communist Party (MCP), complete with images of CTs. (Courtesy Rhodesian African Rifles Regimental Association (UK))

A dead terrorist trussed onto a carrying pole. (Courtesy Rhodesian African Rifles Regimental Association (UK))

aggravated by having the RhAR's presence compromised by RAF Vickers Valetta military transport aircraft activity. The single CT casualty occurred on 20 March, and is contained in patrol commander Corporal Mudingi's report:

The time was 1030 hours and I had reached GR 181748 when the time came for the hourly break. Suddenly Private Munorya (Mor Pl) saw a CT 15–20 yards away to his left front. Both he and the leading scout, Fred (4 Pl), opened fire with their Patchetts simultaneously. The CT was hit, dropped his pack and ran towards the S Kinchin. I shouted at the patrol to charge and saw another CT with a Sten running away. Malinga (4 Pl), the Bren gunner, in the meantime reached the river at the same time as the wounded CT and when the latter jumped in and attempted to swim across, hit him again with several well-directed bursts from the waist. The CT struggled back to the near bank and I shot him with my shotgun. Private Mutambo then grabbed him by the hair and pulled him out as he was sinking. Corporal Chedi (Mor Pl) then said he had seen a third CT. We searched the area thoroughly but could find no trace of the two survivors. We called off the search at 1200 hours, and began to carry the body back to base. At about 1230 hours, I met Lance-Corporal Obert's patrol and sent one man and the CT pack back to report. The dead CT was identified as one Ho Yong of the Endau Food Cultivation Unit.

Boarding an RAF Westland Whirlwind in a jungle clearing. (Courtesy Rhodesian African Rifles Regimental Association (UK))

Barefoot porters, more often than not Sarawak or Sakai, contemplate the seemingly impossible. (Courtesy Rhodesian African Rifles Regimental Association (UK))

THE GREEN HOWARDS LAST ALMA DAY IN MALAYA

By Major D.H. De T. Reade

On September 20, the 1st Battalion the Green Howards will spend their fourth and last Alma Day in Malaya. The Battalion leave for home before Christmas.

'We shall be fully operational on the trail of Communist terrorists,' says the Adjutant, Captain Gordon Wesley. But that evening, as patrols sit in the jungle waiting for night, the normal patrol wireless link with H.Q. will contain a few words of greeting from their C.O. Lieut.-Colonel A.D. Miller.

'At company bases – all are tactical bases – there will be a short silence in memory of our fallen. In Malaya we have lost one officer and 18 other ranks.'

The Green Howards went to Malaya from Khartum, becoming fully operational in October, 1949. [They] ... certainly made their killing powers felt with the Communist terrorists in the Tampin and Malacca areas [south-east of Kuala Lumpur]. They were in the right place at the right time, and their marksmanship was first-class.

Their most important success was achieved by a patrol which killed seven terrorists in the Tampin area. At 6.45pm the patrol (drawn from the machine-gun platoon of support company but naturally without machine-guns) halted. Noises from the bandit camp could be heard plainly. The camp was well in the jungle, seven hours marching inland from the nearest road and over 2,000 feet above sea level.

Captain Nigel Bagnall intended to creep up in the early hours of the morning, but rain began to fall, and he decided that it would cover any noise the patrol might in creeping upon the camp. Before 6am the camp was covered in the Yorkshiremen's sights, and when the surprised bandit sentry who came out for first duty was killed, the Green Howards went in and killed six more, including Chong Pin, the District Secretary of the Tampin Branch.

Captain Bagnall, who won the MC [Military Cross] in October 1950, has led patrols which have accounted for 17 terrorists. Support company is a post-war innovation ... so far it has 19 kills to its credit.

Altogether, the Battalion have killed 93 terrorists. They have been awarded four Military Crosses, three Military Medals, one M.B.E. and 21 Mentions-in-Despatches.

Before the regimental band plays the 'Bonnie English Rose' – the Green Howards' tune – for the last time in Malaya, I hope the Battalion will have had a century of kills chalked up to their credit.

(*Yorkshire Post and Leeds Intelligencer*, Saturday, 30 August 1952)

On 8 June, persistent patrolling by Lieutenant Essex-Clark's platoon finally paid dividends, as he recalls:

One day, after we'd had a successful night ambush, the director of operations in Malaya, Lieutenant-General Sir Roger Bower, told us that he 'needed desperately' a 'captured enemy person', and that whoever caught one would be immediately decorated.

My platoon was patrolling in some badly maintained and scrub-carpeted mature rubber. The afternoon curfew for rubber tappers was in force. The askari were looking for signs of CT meetings with the local supporters and sympathisers, the Min Yuen. Normally each of my three section patrols would search areas in which the natural features could indicate the possible presence of CT. On this occasion, the sections had been 'fanned' out geometrically from the platoon base to search triangular sectors. All three section patrols were moving 500 metres from the base, each separated by 120 degrees, then turning 60 degrees right for 500 metres before turning 60 degrees right again and returning to the base before starting off again on another compass bearing. We called this the 'clock-ray' method of searching an area and we used it to search a grid square per day (almost 8,000 square metres) in featureless terrain such as swamps and some rubber plantations.

Inventories of foodstuffs and utensils found in captured CT camps helped define the enemy. (Courtesy Rhodesian African Rifles Regimental Association (UK))

The late afternoon storm clouds were building up and the pleasant dappled shade from the mature rubber trees had given way to grey-green gloom. Tabuya's section was patrolling north-west and when, at the end of his outward leg, he heard the plantation water pump 'tump-tump-tumpetty-tumping' merrily in the distance, he decided to investigate. He rounded a spur and saw a corrugated-iron-roofed pump shed. It was about 100 metres from where the jungle met the rubber plantation and he could smell the sour odour of old latex mixed with the fumes from the pump. He paused to size up the shed carefully before approaching. As his section was in 'open' rubber, he had put them in an arrow-head formation. His two-man Bren group was his right wing on the marginally higher ground, a scout was at the arrow point and he was in the centre with his four-man rifle group on his left. They froze as he went forward with his scout, Matias, to have a closer peek. Tabuya and Matias watched, prone, for a few minutes.

They were about to go forward again when they saw five khaki-clad CT armed with rifles and Sten guns, coming very slowly and cautiously out of the jungle. The CT paused and then furtively crept towards the shed. Because Tabuya's men were in rubber, they had not cocked their weapons. They were forbidden to do so in case we, or any member of the security forces, accidentally shot a rubber tapper. We could cock our weapons only when in contact with the CT who in this case, were now about 70 metres away and might have heard our patrol doing so.

Tabuya, cleverly anticipating sound and distance, pulled back the section of his brand-new 'user trial' FN 7.62mm self-loading rifle to the 'tump' of the pump and let it slap forward with the next 'tumpetty'. The others followed suit. Tabuya and Matias slipped into the drainage ditch and crawled through the mud closer to the shed. The leading CT was about 30 metres away. Tabuya gently nuzzled his rifle forward through the grass on the edge of the ditch and took aim. The terrorist stood next to a tree near the shed and paused. He turned towards Tabuya, started and was shot through the chest. The other four scrambled off, ducking and weaving through the scrubby rubber. As Tabuya said afterwards, it was like 'chasing the wind'. Corporal Taderera's section saw the group and fired from about 150 metres away but the enemy changed direction and disappeared over a ridge towards the jungle edge.

Up on the hill at the platoon base Pisayi had gone forward over the crest with three men of the platoon headquarters to investigate. Suddenly he sprang off like a jack rabbit, the others following. Rifle shots and 9mm Sten-gun bursts were fired and many grenades crunched venomously. Undeterred by shots from three CTs and grenades from another, and remembering only the general's challenging words, he chased after one of them as relentlessly as a lion singling out his kill. Pisayi was no sprinter but he doggedly ran his quarry down until exhausted and then tackled him to the ground. After quickly handing him to his three askari companions, Pisayi, again under fire, chased down another. Two got away.

Improvised river crossing, but unusable when flooding. (Courtesy Rhodesian African Rifles Regimental Association (UK))

Captured Communist terrorists. (Courtesy Rhodesian African Rifles Regimental Association (UK))

REDS GO BACK TO JUNGLE

Talks between Malayan Communists and Government representatives broke up in failure today, though there was hope that fresh talks might take place later.

Chin Peng, leader of 3,500 Communists, drove back into the jungle after saying: 'We will never accept surrender at any time and will continue our struggle to the last man.'

The cause of the breakdown of the talks, which it was hoped would bring an end to the eight-year-old jungle war, was the Communist refusal to accept investigation of their loyalty, which they identified with surrender. The alternative to the loyalty test was repatriation to Communist China.

Today, at the final session of the two-day talks at Baling, near the border of Thailand, Chin Peng said the Communists would lay down their arms if the federal Government of Malaya took over from Britain complete control of internal security and all the armed forces in the country.

Tengku (Prince) Abdul Rahman, Chief Minister of Malaya, said afterwards that Chin Peng had told him he could not discuss matters further because he had gone as far as his mandate allowed. The Tengku, who said the Communists wanted to save face, added that tomorrow he would announce that his Government's amnesty offer, made last September to the Communist terrorists, would end in one month's time.

Mr David Marshall, Singapore Chief Minister, told Chin Peng that the welfare of 7,000,000 people in Malaya came before 3,000 Communist terrorists. He appealed to the Communists to sacrifice their pride.

(*Aberdeen Evening Express*, Thursday, 29 December 1955)

The dead CT was identified as Yee Pow of the Bekok communist branch. One of the captured was Mok Cheong of 32 Independent Platoon, later sentenced to death; the other was Chan Ser Hock of the Labis branch.

Essex-Clark continues:

Later they found the packs of five CTs concealed just inside the jungle-rubber edge. They had been looking for a message from the Min Yuen in the shed. The second terrorist captured had been wounded by us in a night ambush in a palm oil plantation months before. We had hit and severely damaged his right hand and that was why he was only throwing grenades.

The general now had his 'captured enemy persons'. Pisayi was awarded the Military Medal for bravery [see Chapter 8] and 8 Platoon was very proud because we now had the highest number of 'kills and captures' of any platoon in Malaya. I was happy, but also disappointed. During this magnificent action by my platoon, I had been immaculately dressed and carrying a sword on the Padang in Kuala Lumpur. I was commanding the Rhodesian contingent at the last Queen's Birthday Parade held in Malaya. Fred Harrison phoned me that evening, illegally, but told me what had happened in veiled speech. For obvious security reasons there should have been no mention of the detail of the captured CT until their intelligence was exhausted. I found out the detail of the contact when, much later, I had to put on a live demonstration for the delighted general!

In March 1947, a 17-year-old Frank Walker enlisted as a regular soldier with the 1st Battalion, the Prince of Wales's Own West Yorkshire Regiment. In October that year, Walker arrived in

Captured Communist terrorists being questioned. (Courtesy Rhodesian African Rifles Regimental Association (UK))

No. 194 Squadron RAF Westland WS-51 Dragonfly helicopter, made under licence in the UK as a version of the American Sikorsky S-51. (Courtesy Jonathan Pittaway)

Malaya on his first tour of duty. In May 1948, he was transferred to Austria, before completing a second Malayan tour of duty from 1953 to 1955, now with the rank of staff sergeant. After serving in Northern Ireland, Singapore, Gibraltar, Berlin, Cyprus, Belfast and Canada, Lieutenant Colonel Frank Walker retired from the British army in 1996.

Now living in a care home in Northampton, in an exclusive interview with the author, Lieutenant Colonel Walker spoke of some of his experiences:

My regiment was officially based at Ipoh [in the State of Perak, western Malaya], from where the battalion was split up to various parts of Malaya.

We had with us a squadron of Gurkhas, as well as a dog admin unit. The dogs were used for tracking, and damn good they were too, especially when they had proper trackers with them. These barefoot men came from Sarawak in Borneo, and were attached to battalions operating in Malaya – invaluable, very, very good. They would love the night-attack patrols. You put together one of their patrols with one of our dog handlers – that was your best hope because that was how they worked, at night.

I only went on one night ambush, but it was a good one. We killed three leaders. The taxi driver, who we were after, was the reason why we were laying the ambush. They were using the taxis to pick up these supplies, and they were mad enough to know that where they were, we would be. Our people didn't put much to it, but as time went by they began to realise how good an ambush it had been.

The information that had been given to our warriors was that this meeting was going to take place at this time – just before Christmas. They were going to pick up loads of medical supplies, and two days before Christmas was when it was meant to be.

Commanding officer of the SAS in Malaya, Lieutenant-Colonel John 'Tod' Sloane, arrives in an RAF Dragonfly helicopter on a visit to the troops in the jungle. (Courtesy Jonathan Pittaway)

It was just off a normal straight road. We were offloaded, for ambush purposes, on the right-hand side, if you can visualise that. The road was coming down this way [showing with his hands] with the jungle on the right-hand side.

The taxi driver would have all these supplies in the back of his vehicle. People in the local community, who had been on our side, had picked up information that these people were going to come that night. We were on the right-hand side of the road alongside a Malayan Railways line and we had been told that they were going to come down the road and cross the railway line in one particular spot.

We laid up the whole day before in a very small wood to set this ambush so that no one would see us. There were fifteen of us altogether, split into small groups. The middle one was one man short – he was our company commander.

I was armed with a rifle because that is what I wanted. It was a Lee Enfield .303, modernised for Malaya, and called a jungle carbine. We had a Bren gun with each ambush position – we were well armed. The order was given that should we see anything we knew to be logically the enemy, someone would give the order [to spring the ambush] by firing a shot off, or get down, or what have you.

Our position was alongside the railway, pointing out to a sawmill, which had a light on the top. In conjunction with local people, if they could see anything, they would flick the light. It was the right place to be.

When they opened this ambush, I was in the last position on the right. On that side, we could see these people coming in with their patrol, and of course, they were coming through so brazenly because they didn't know we were there, you know. When we opened the ambush, all hell let loose, as you can imagine. They fired towards us and came in front of the railway, crossing the railway line at an angle in front of my guys. My left-hand shot let fly because he saw them. I saw what I knew to be a girl, that's how bloody close they were.

'WOODEN HORSE' OFFICER KILLED IN MALAYA

Royal Air Force 'planes went out today in search of 40 guerrillas who ambushed and killed 12 police and civilians, including Mr Michael Clinton Codner, one of three British officers who made the 'Wooden Horse' escape from a German prison camp. [Lieutenant Michael Codner, Flight Lieutenant Eric Williams and Flight Lieutenant Oliver Philpot escaped from the German POW camp, Stalag Luft III, on the evening of 19 October 1943, via a 100-foot tunnel that had taken the three men three months to dig.]

Four guerrillas were reported killed and four wounded in a battle after the ambush near Tanjong Malim, in the Perak-Selangor border area. It was one of the worst incidents in Malaya's three-and-a-half-year-old emergency.

The dead included eight police, Mr W.H. Fourniss, a public works engineer, a Chinese and a Malay. The guerrillas struck when the police and civilians were going to repair a sabotaged water pipeline on a rubber estate. They attacked with Bren guns, Sten guns, rifles and grenades. The leading members of the police and civilian party were killed outright, but surviving police returned the fire until relief arrived.

Police Lieutenant W. Jones led 15 police reinforcements who arrived 20 minutes after the ambush. He found three wounded Malay policemen shooting it out from exposed ground against a greatly superior number of men concealed in surrounding bracken.

Lieutenant Jones came under fire as he crossed a river bridge. He dropped his gun and jumped into the river. Then he climbed out, recovered his gun, and with his party drove off the attackers.

One police Bren-gunner fired off two magazines before he was killed. Every armed policeman in the ambushed party was killed or wounded.

Mr Codner, an Assistant District Officer at Tanjong Malim, joined the Malayan Civil Service in 1950 ... aged 31, [he] was married in September 1948 to Miss Rosemary Mosley Leigh. A son was born to Mrs Codner last September in Bungsar Hospital, Kuala Lumpur.

(*Yorkshire Post and Leeds Intelligencer*, Wednesday, 26 March 1952)

There were eight of them. Of course, they let fly with everything they had and ran like hell. We didn't lose anybody, because there was so much chaos going on at this stage, everybody took to the low ground.

Eventually I was in a position to say stop firing, because I could see there was nothing going on around us. We up sticks and start running after these people, which was useless, as they knew exactly where they were going.

We found out the next day when we were covering the ground again, that they had come right across the road, exactly where they should, to meet up with this taxi with the medical supplies. During the post mortem we decided to find out how many shots had been fired. It turned out, a helluva lot. The taxi was still there, absolutely full of bloody bullet holes, and the driver was killed. Pity really, because he was one of our informers. He was doing this as a second job. But we took it that he was working for both sides.

Lance Corporal Frank Walker of the Prince of Wales's West Yorkshire Regiment. (Courtesy Lieutenant Colonel Frank Walker)

The chaps came out the next morning with the sergeant major – he in his Ferret [scout car] coming along these bloody tracks, right alongside the railway line. We were trying to guide him because he was only this far away from this massive sink-hole. In fact he almost did tip over into it. His left-hand wheels went over the lip of the sink-hole, so we had to stop the whole thing. It was hanging over the side by two wheels – a big drop. Oh and the sergeant major was crapping himself thinking he was a goner. We managed to get it out, using rope from the vehicle that was coming behind. He was a very relieved sergeant major.

For most security force patrols, the norm was ten- to twenty-day patrols, painfully and frustratingly characterised by fruitless footslogging through undulating jungle terrain – day upon day of an ennui-filled existence.

Deployed into the Sungei Spang Loi area on a twenty-day patrol commencing 31 October 1951, Lieutenant Essex-Clark's platoon set off to search for Hor Lung's 32 Independent Platoon of the MRLA, which, based on weak information, was moving into the area after brutal terrorist activity in the adjacent rubber estates. Hor Lung was a politburo member in charge of the southern operations of the MPLA since 1953. There was nothing there, however, except 'swamps, rising creeks, more swamps and no evidence of CT activity'.

At the end of the patrol, the platoon had had one kill. Essex-Clark's personal diary gives a remarkable insight into the not untypical experiences of the British and Commonwealth ground forces in Malaya during the emergency:

Wednesday 31st October 1956
Based up near Pt 38 on the mosquito and leech riddled Spang Loi River. That Court Welch was to immortalise with his sarcastic poem 'By the leptospirosial waters of the flowing Spang Loi'.

Thursday 1st November
Patrolled extensively all day in the miserable Buloh Kassap swamp area. NTR [nothing to report]. No evidence of CT camp areas or any areas suitable for CT staging camps. The water is filthy, slurpy and still. Heard on the news that the Brits have bombed targets in the Suez

C Squadron, SAS, Humber Scout car, Malaya. (Courtesy Jonathan Pittaway)

Silent radio-watch in the Malayan jungle. (Courtesy Rhodesian African Rifles Regimental Association (UK))

Canal areas in Egypt. I hope this doesn't lead to a third world war for our families' sakes. Rained 'cats and dogs' overnight and none of the platoon could sleep for the thunderous rain, and incessant croaking by frogs.

Sunday 2nd November
Rain still thundering down and the creeks and swamps are rising. Rations arrived for 4 Platoon D Coy = Callsign 31, David Heppenstall. David and his platoon looked a bit sodden and David was unimpressed with our wasted patrolling efforts. Rained thunderously again late afternoon and evening – there's not much dry clothing or un-sodden areas for a decent basha anymore. NTR.

Monday 5th November
An SEP (Surrendered Enemy Person) told Special Branch that Hor Lung is still coming our way. Captain Dudley Rowell our 2iC, with Maj Bill Godwin on a majors' course in Singapore, went out sick this morning back across the Muar. I am now in command of the company. There's not much happening so there's very little command responsibility. The Palong is still rising and we may have to move tomorrow. Guy Fawkes day, believe it or not. NTR again.

Sergeant Billy Conn, C Squadron, SAS, communicating from the middle of a Malayan rice paddy field. (Courtesy Craig Fourie)

Tuesday 6th November
We were sent to ambush likely crossings on the Palong River to prevent Hor Lung escaping into the Huge Rengam State Forest Area. We (C Coy) were given about 3,000 yards of the swelling and rising Palong to watch. So we split up into three ambush points per platoon. That means we were watching only about one tenth of our allotted responsibility. The chances of Hor Lung bumping into us were as good as finding a friend, who didn't want to be found, at King's Cross Railway Station during evening rush hour. Bloody remote!

While moving north we were excited to see footprints at a creek crossing where we were delayed and two shots were fired at us as we bunched at the creek. I'd forgotten my adage that while crossing any obstacle such as a creek or fallen tree, we should move at a slow speed past that crossing for the length of our platoon column, about 125 yards at a 5 yd spacing per man, by not doing so, the rear of our column had to speed up and when we stopped it caused bunching.

On shot hit Pte Taswivinga's pack and knocked him down (only his pride was hurt). The lead section Cpl Tabuya and I charged into the area from where we thought the shots were fired and found nothing but more footprints, which were soon obliterated by the heavy rain. There were only two CT involved so I knew that it was not Hor Lung's mob but probably couriers going to meet him. I stopped and reported this incident back to Bn HQ. We continued to our new ambush positions and waited. Hor Lung must be still west of us on the other side of the Palong!

Wednesday 7th November
Moved further north to ambush positions on possible but not probable crossing places on the east bank of the cruddy and scrubby banks of the Palong. Nothing but the odd whooping gibbons, more mosquitoes and leeches, placed my small ambush gp Pl HQ and 3 section (Cpl Jere) near a watering spot for wild pigs and settled down. It's hard to keep alert or stop being wearily bored. NTR.

Thursday 8th November
The coy moved to new northern positions on the left or west bank of the Palong. Casevaced Pte Chamunorwa from Fred's 9 pl . Flt Lt Ron Kerr came in onto our orange 'Tango' on a

An RAF Douglas DC-3 Dakota rations airdrop. (Courtesy Rhodesian African Rifles Regimental Association (UK))

SKYMEN OUT IN MALAYA RAID

Biggest Joint Attack on Terrorists

The Royal Air Force today dropped hundreds of paratroopers into the jungle near Ipoh, Northern Malaya, in 'Operation Termite', the biggest joint Army-Air operation undertaken against the Malayan terrorists. Lincoln bombers first softened up the area with thousands of pounds of high explosives.

The Malayan Communist Party is believed to have its headquarters in the dense jungle east of Ipoh, and one of the most notorious leaders, Chin Peng, is supposed to be hiding in there.

An official Government reporter aboard one of the Valetta dropping planes said: 'The entire operation was shrouded in the greatest secrecy until zero hour. Six Valettas of 48 Squadron R.A.F. took off from the Federation capital of Kuala Lumpur loaded with troops of the 22nd Special Air Service Regiment.'

A Reuter representative in one of the Valetta paratroop planes cables: 'The joint bombing and parachute operation went off with absolute precision. If there were Communist terrorists below, the paratroopers must have got them.'

Troops were dropped in 'sticks' of five on to jungle believed to be the thickest in Malaya. Giant trees poke out of the jungle more than 200 feet above the ground. Daylight seldom reaches the damp gloomy jungle floor.

Men of the Special Air Service, who developed the technique for building jungle forts in areas where there are no roads, wear thick clothing and crash helmets. When their parachutes catch in the top branches they unwind a strong silken cord and let themselves down in spider-like fashion with sub-machine guns at the ready.

(*Sunderland Daily Echo and Shipping Gazette*, Thursday, 8 July 1954)

---

higher sandbank in an RAF Bristol Sycamore to pick him up. The Sycamore has dangerously low blades in the front while idling, especially while sinking into the wet sand! The Palong is still rising. Chamunorwa had slashed his leg badly with a panga while preparing an ambush position.

We then learn from Bn HQ that a big search for Hor Lung from the south on the west side of the Palong has started – and we (all of C Coy) are to cross the Palong to search for his base. We will start doing so near what Special Branch tells us is an apparent old wooden bridge near a resettled overgrown kampong on the west bank. I patrol north and find the old bridge, which is now only almost covered poles in the fast moving Palong water. I decide that only Yvo's and my platoon will cross with our platoon's toggle-ropes along the old poles to get on the far side before last light to start our search at 'sparrow-fart' tomorrow. We do so with many dangerous moments, and are based up in a two-platoon base in primary jungle on the far side of the Palong by last-light. NTR on the evening sked [schedule] except to tell HQ where we are and that we would start our search at first light the next day.

I decide that clock-ray patrolling tomorrow will be useless to find a CT base camp quickly, and decide to try parallel echelon patrolling from a north–south start-line and groups

Above: Unappetising field rations. (Courtesy Rhodesian African Rifles Regimental Association (UK))

Right: A C Squadron SAS paratrooper being checked by a member of the RAF. (Courtesy Jonathan Pittaway)

50 metres apart along the start line to move due west (270°). We pause for a minute after every five minutes patrol westward, using the six sections that I had so we will either find his 20-man trail if he was moving past us, and bump into him if he wasn't. I also felt from what I had seen of old deserted CT camps that they were nearly always on a high spur line next to a creek or swamp water, and our various routes would be near many of those.

Friday 9th November

This was our 'BIG' day. We moved out into our parallel echelon position north of our base, leaving at first light (about 0630 hrs) and start parallel movement 30 minutes later, leaving the signallers and batmen plus our CSM Reg Griffiths in the base, At 0939 hrs there was a roar of small-arms fire and grenades, which meant that we'd bumped into CT because we did not carry grenades. The CT scattered (bomb-shelled!) and all our five other groups took up their stay-put static ambush positions including mine on a spur next to a swampy creek (Sungei Senama on the map), and soon our three-man group saw and heard CT scuttling and chattering on the opposite spur. We fired at them and they exchanged fire, and we chased them until they got away from us. We found blood smeared on some sapling trunks.

When back at our patrol-base I learnt that Cpl Munyameni of 7 Pl had shot and killed a big gold-toothed CT carrying a Sten gun; so we reported our contact to Bn HQ with a 'ho-hum' reaction when I asked for a chopper to take out the body. The Whirlwind RAF chopper came in on a small overgrown Lallang patch on the Palong side of the old Sakai kampong we had based away from last night. It also brought in two RAVC dog teams from the SWB [South Wales Borderers] and their HQ company commander, who was an absolute

Permanently soaked, here unloading weapons from wooden dugout canoes. (Courtesy Rhodesian African Rifles Regimental Association (UK))

delight, and showed much interest in the tactics of echelon parallel and creel line patrolling. He left with the CT body but left Lt Ken Green, SWB, with us and the two dog teams. So we immediately got our patrols to go with the dog teams and I took them to my Senama contact area where there were still two new faint blood trails, from hands on branches, new drag marks, and another highly burnished Sten gun with a half-loaded magazine. We followed the blood and tracks until the rain again thundered down and washed the blood and footprints away. I checked the Sten and it fired well.

We are elated we've got the battalion's first kill since we'd arrived in Malaya on 26th April: nearly seven months ago. [See Essex-Clark's alternate account on pages 94–97.]

Saturday 10th November
Follow-up patrols moving into the likely areas of the CT moving east and over the Palong into hides in the Rengam State Forest. We search mainly along stream and creeks and looking for spurs that could hide a 19 CT group with wounded. Other battalions, apparently, and the rest of the RhAR are searching near villages in the rubber plantations well south-west of us in case the CT want to get their wounded into some medical care on the edge of the jungle and rubber. We find nothing with our nine section patrols. NTR.

HELICOPTERS OFF TO MALAYA JUNGLE WAR

Britain's first offensive helicopter squadron leaves Gosport this week to help to take the Malaya jungle war right on to the terrorist's doorstep.

It is fulfilling the promise of General Sir Gerald Templer, Malaya's anti-bandit chief, that early next year 'we shall have helicopters in the jungle which will enable us to move troops quickly to trouble spots requiring fast reinforcement, in areas deep in the jungle.' Thus, Sir Gerald added, 'several days of gruelling overland march by troops would be avoided.'

A little after two months from the time they arrived in Britain by sea from America under the mutual aid programme, the 10 Sikorsky HRS2 helicopters ['Whirlwind'] of 848 Squadron, Gosport – the first naval front-line helicopter squadron to be formed – will be shipped aboard the aircraft-carrier Perseus this week. The Perseus sails for Malaya 'very shortly'.

The HRS2, the biggest helicopter flying in Britain today, can carry eight fully armed troops in addition to two pilots – or three stretcher cases and three walking wounded, plus crew.

Because training the squadron has been such a rush job – many of the ground crew at least had never seen a helicopter before they moved to Gosport four weeks ago – few of the men have a clear picture of what they can expect in Malaya, but to prepare for the jungle war, flying training in the last two weeks had included 'jungle operations' in the New Forest.

In the difficult operations in the jungle many pilots believe they may have to make their own landing grounds themselves, possibly even by blasting the jungle from the air with bombs before they can land.

(*Yorkshire Evening Post*, Monday, 8 December 1952)

Sunday 11th November

What a day! We took the company airdrop on a tiny DZ. Stuff everywhere and two packs in high trees! Also an airdrop and helicopter were trying to use the DZ/LZ [Drop Zone/ Landing Zone] at the same time. We casevaced Yvo in an RAF Whirlwind with a raging fever (Leptospirosis?) and sent out the dog teams and Lt Green in the same helicopter. We also learnt that Lt John Borden (RAN) a South African naval helicopter pilot that I'd got to know well, has been killed in a helicopter crash.

'Buttons' Wells-West and Graeme McKenzie's platoons from A Company linked up with us this afternoon (for the record I am now commanding and responsible for five platoons of 1RAR – 2,3, 7, 8 and 9. All settled down later and is quiet in my five-platoon base, but I certainly enjoyed my rum ration in my mug of tea this afternoon. We had a quiet night smothered in insect repellent while we chatted and sipped our tea through stand-to and then covered by our mosquito nets, which we could not use even at night while in our ambush positions.

We now had a rather secure five-platoon patrol base and feel very secure. CO said we would be out on Monday and to get ready for the rugby match against the SWB at Segamat on the next Saturday afternoon. I'll have to get him ready! All the officers and one cpl from C Coy are in the team.

Monday 12th November

We were told our lift out was delayed until tomorrow. As we'd just got resupplied they then delayed our lift for a few more days. We got the dog teams and Lt Green out by helicopter by 1230 hrs and our two-company group patrolled further along the west bank and then the north end of the Palong loop to the west to see if they could find a spot where the CT might have crossed. Now that the river had subsided we find sand banks on the north loop that the CT could have used. We also continued patrols towards the Rengam State Forest, the likely CT hiding area, but, apart from reporting the sandbanks, no evidence of a crossing, so again, NTR.

Tuesday 13th November to Saturday 17th November

We (all five pls) continue patrolling further eastwards into the Rengam State Forest from our base which is now on the east bank of the Palong, for another five NTR days moving our patrol base each day, to when our rations expired. There was no sign of CT at all during our spur and creek-line patrolling.

Sunday 18th November

We learn on the morning sked that we are that that we are to be air-lifted out of LZ MILNER (old Kampong Menonngol) at 0700 hrs the next day. So during the day we have a 5 hr jungle bash for 2,300 yds back to the LZ and crossed back over the now exposed sand banks of a now sluggish Palong and readied ourselves for flying out tomorrow from the big LZ on Kampong Menonngol, an old resettled, deserted, and derelict kampong. We get the LZ ready with the fluorescent orange 'T' panel and the water for the lithium hydride to produce the hydrogen for our marker balloon on the side of the LZ, then sun ourselves while basing up comfortably around this wide open LZ this afternoon. NTR.

White-smoke grenade marking a helicopter landing zone, or LZ. (Courtesy Rhodesian African Rifles Regimental Association (UK))

Monday 19th November

By 0630hrs we were ready and in our helicopter groups. The three helicopters came in at 0659 hrs and I marshalled the first aircraft onto the panel. Flt Lt Cooper, RAF, then took over the marshalling duty after he arrived in the first aircraft. All went smoothly until the process paused for a long time (nearly an hour) for helicopter refuelling at our destination LZ and one of Graeme McKenzie's askari decided hysterically to run off into the jungle. Fortunately, we had enough time to collect him and bring him back before all our extraction was complete. He thought that he was being left behind! It was a bit embarrassing having some of the RWF officers and men with us, but he was soon found and brought back to join his section and airlift group.

Unfortunately, Brit (C of A) airworthiness specs stated that the RAF Westland Whirlwinds (*mukacepu*) were not allowed to carry the same number of troops as the Royal Navy Sikorsky S55s (*chikasaws*), which were not so restricted and to which we had been accustomed. So we had to reshuffle our groups to match the RAF requirements, which also meant that as the fuel load dropped they could carry more. So it was a bit disorganised and a bit of silly shuffling, but all went well and we were all back at our destination on time to meet our road convoy to take us back to Labis, and A Coy pls back to Cha'ah.

We were replaced by A and B Coys of the Royal Welsh Fusiliers [RWF], after leaving Flt Lt Cooper and my CSM Reg Griffiths to handle helicopter movement and loading airlift out and the RWF airlift in. I handed over my responsibilities to OC of A Coy RWF (Major Eggleton). He was expecting a major not a lieutenant. We (80 pax) were all out, and they were all in, in

28 journeys using three RAF Whirlwinds. We were landed at LZ LUTON in a space in the rubber near Ladang Geddes by 1200 hrs.

Tuesday 20th November
Started training at Cha'ah for the rugby game against the SWB next Friday 23rd November at Segamat. I officially reported my contact details in a detailed written report and discussion with three RhAR senior officers, but not the CO Lt Col Jock Anderson who was still absent

FINAL NOTE
In the rugby game against the SWB we were well beaten, but held our own courageously but unskilfully, by their rugby team masquerading as their Signals Platoon, by 23 to 0.

I reported my contact details, and tactics that were well outside of the ATOM [Anti-Terrorist Operations in Malaya] Pamphlet doctrine, to Frank Fitzgerald (Bn 2iC) who, with Maj Don Mitchell (OC HQ Coy) and the pompous John Shaw (IO) were uninterested. Fitzgerald said that it was just luck, and Mitchell's comment was 'how mundane'. Shaw just sneered condescendingly. I was congratulated by no one except Bill Godwin for the battalion's and our company's first kill. After all the elation from the short successful moments of combat, I felt very flat indeed!

So ended a twenty-day patrol in Malaya. My platoon got another kill and capture nine months later, with *maningi* [an African language word meaning 'many' or 'a lot of'] patrolling in the *ulu* in between. So it was no action-packed tour of Malaya from 1956 to 1958.

Nevertheless, I captained the 1RAR cross-country team to win the FARELF Unit Cross Country Championship beating the confident and cocky Cheshire regiment team that had won

Essex-Clark marshalling an RAF Westland Whirlwind to start an extraction from a resettled and cleared old *kampong* area (Kampong Menonngol) on the Palong River (Sungei Palong) in Johore province. (Courtesy Brigadier John 'Digger' Essex-Clark)

The QUEEN has been graciously pleased to give orders, as on the 30th August, 1957, for the following appointments to the Most Excellent Order of the British Empire, in recognition of distinguished service in Malaya, during the period ending on that date:

To be Additional Officers of the Military Division of the said Most Excellent Order:"

Lieutenant-Colonel John ANDERSON

Recommendation citation as endorsed by General Charles Keightley, Commander-in-Chief, Far East Land Forces:

During the year that the 1st Bn The Rhodesian African Rifles have been in Malaya Lt Col ANDERSON has commanded his Battalion with outstanding ability. The Battalion came inexperienced to operations against Communist Terrorists but very soon the Battalion showed the results of careful training and spirited direction by the Commanding Officer.

Because of their flair for tracking and silent movement the Battalion had been to a great extent employed in the deep jungle where their natural ability has been made full use of. Whilst the Communist Terrorists avoid security forces it becomes increasingly difficult to gain many successes against them in the deep jungle.

Intensive patrolling carried out for long periods without any contact with the Communist Terrorists has been maintained relentlessly. Lacking contacts to sharpen their keenness and efficiency it might be expected that frustration would tend to cause morale to drop in the Battalion. This has been very far from the case. Inspired by Lt Col ANDERSON's confidence in his men to prove their worth in action against the enemy and with his enthusiasm and drive, morale has risen steadily.

Eventually after much patient work in the deep jungle excellent successes were gained which displayed the Battalion's great dash and eagerness to close with the enemy.

The Commanding Officer himself has taken part in many reconnaissances in the search for Communist Terrorists. Imbued with the determination to eliminate the enemy the Battalion has followed his lead magnificently. When the situation at last allowed the Battalion to operate in the area they know best they have had two recent and highly successful actions. Great courage, determination and outstanding skill in minor tactics and field craft were shown.

Morale in the Battalion could not be higher. The keenness and enthusiasm of all ranks is exhilarating. Lt Col ANDERSON has proved himself an outstanding and courageous Commander whose personality is truly reflected in his Battalion. He is the ideal Commander of the 1st Bn The Rhodesian African Rifles and the leadership he has given has firmly established their reputation as a most successful operational Battalion in Malaya.

(*London Gazette*, 20 December 1957 and WO/208)

the NATO championship in Germany the previous year. I also commanded the 1RAR contingent on the last Queen's Birthday parade in Kuala Lumpur. Played rugby and captained the Gurkha Division Rugby team that won the FARELF Rugby Championships, and played cricket for the FARELF XI against various teams; and with Sgt Gondocondo came second in the FARELF small arms and Bren LMG competition in Singapore – no wonder that I was unpopular!

7. WINNERS AND LOSERS

As early as 1950, it had certainly become apparent to the British media that, by simple interpretation of the statistics, Britain's fiscus was under tremendous strain putting out fires in, amongst others, Palestine, Berlin and Malaya. Military success measured in terms of kill rates as a ratio to loss of own forces made uncomfortable, if not tragic, reading. And when armies collide, civilians are always the losers, especially when it is their 'freedom' that is being fought over. The killing of twenty-four unarmed villagers by British troops on 12 December 1948 – the so-called Batang Kali massacre – highlighted the Catch-22 situation that had become a way of life for many Malayan civilians.

The Scotsman's correspondent in Singapore analysed the situation in September 1950. The latest figures had revealed that in the previous two and a quarter years 1,385 CTs had been killed and 1,064 civilians murdered. By adding some 600 members of the security forces, including police, and a further 400 civilians missing, to the civilian tally, 'thus bringing the bandit score to more than 2,000, which is more than the number of terrorists killed and captured'.

Commanding officers switch over. On the left, Lieutenant Colonel Jock Anderson, 1RhAR, arrives in Singapore, where he bids farewell to the departing Lieutenant Colonel G.H.W. Goode DSO, OBE of the 1st Battalion, the Northern Rhodesian Regiment. (Courtesy Rhodesian African Rifles Regimental Association (UK))

During the month of August that year alone, 67 terrorists were eliminated, compared to 87 servicemen and civilians killed and missing. The authorities registered 174 major bandit incidents during the month, against 145 in the January. Included in this figure were 60 ambushes and attacks on vehicles. One bus company in central Malaya had a total of seven buses torched, and at least one insurance company had stopped providing road operators with cover in terms of the Riot and Civil Disobedience Clause.

'Taxes' collected from sympathisers or extorted from unwilling donors was rumoured to be 'as much as £3,000,000 a year'. On face value this seemed wild speculation, but it was never refuted or dismissed as fantasy.

Public opinion, therefore, tended to agree with Commissioner General Malcolm MacDonald who was quoted as saying, 'Only a fool would say the situation is getting better', a comment that was at direct variance with High Commissioner Sir Henry Gurney who believed that there was no doubt that the government was making good progress in 'the bandit war'. A year later, Gurney himself would perish in a CT ambush near Fraser's Hill on the Kuala Kubu Road.

During the emergency, 1,346 Malayan troops and police, and 519 British military personnel lost their lives. There were 2,406 wounded.

From the Commonwealth contingents, thirty-nine Australians were killed and twenty-seven wounded. The New Zealanders lost fifteen, but only three in action – the remainder the crew of a Bristol Freighter that flew into a mountain in 1956. The Southern Rhodesians lost eight and Fiji twenty-five in combat.

Of the Communist terrorists, 6,710 were killed, 1,289 wounded, 1,287 captured and 2,702 surrendered.

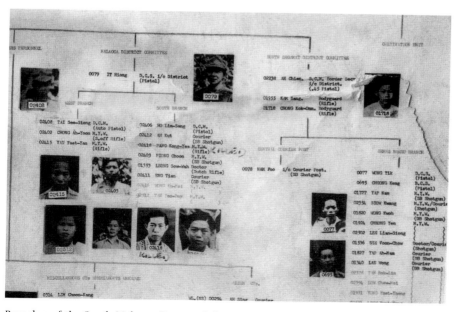

Branches of the South Malayan Bureau of the MCP, prepared by Special Branch. Individual weapons are also shown. (Courtesy Rhodesian African Rifles Regimental Association (UK))

Civilian casualties numbered 2,478 killed and 810 missing.

There was no ceasefire. 'Running Dogs' was the derogatory term used by the Malayan Communists when referring to the British and those of the colony's population who remained loyal to Britain.

With the independence of Malaya on 31 August 1957, the Communists' raison d'être for their 'liberation struggle' evaporated. The last significant engagement with CTs took place in a swamp in the Telok Anson area of Perak in 1958, resulting in the guerrillas surrendering. Small, scattered groups of CTs sought refuge across the Thai border and further afield.

On 31 July 1960, the state of emergency was declared over. MRC leader Chin Peng left Thailand for Beijing, where the Chinese International Liaison Bureau provided him and other Southeast Asian revolutionaries with a roof over their heads. Seven years later, the incorrigible Chin Peng renewed his struggle against the Malaysian government. This chapter in Malaysian history finally closed in 1989.

The author asked Malayan veteran Brigadier John 'Digger' Essex-Clark who, in his informed opinion and based on personal active service in the peninsula, were the winners and who were the losers. His succinct response encapsulates that which was known as the Malayan Emergency.

It was often hard to see by lonely army platoon and SAS troop commanders, from regiment after regiment, from the armies of the UK and the British Commonwealth, from Australia, New Zealand, Rhodesia and Fiji plus the Malay police, what was being achieved by the constant aggressive patrolling of village areas, deep jungle, mangroves and swamps, mountains, valleys and hills.

G.S. MEDALS FOR MALAY SERVICE

A White Paper today announces the award of Naval General Service Medal and General Service Medal (Army and R.A.F.) each with appropriate clasp for service in Malaya since June 16, 1948.

For Naval service afloat the qualification will be 28 days' service patrolling off Malayan coast in support of anti-bandit operations. For Naval service ashore, the qualifying period will be one day or more on duty attached to other eligible forces or police.

Army and R.A.F. qualifications will be one day or more on posted strength of a unit or formations stationed in the Federation of Malaya or the Colony of Singapore.

Ceylon pioneers, Ceylonese locally enlisted, and Indian medical personnel enlisted for service with Army, may also qualify, as may members of Malayan forces and British Red Cross, Naafi [the Navy, Army and Air Force Institutes] and other specified uniformed civilians.

The medal is also awarded to civilians with 28 days' service in Ferret Force or Civil Liaison Corps, and recruits from Sarawak: and to police with three months' service.

Foreign nationals, for instance Chinese, will, be eligible subject to approved conditions.

The ribbon will be issued shortly.

(*Gloucestershire Echo*, Tuesday, 21 March 1950)

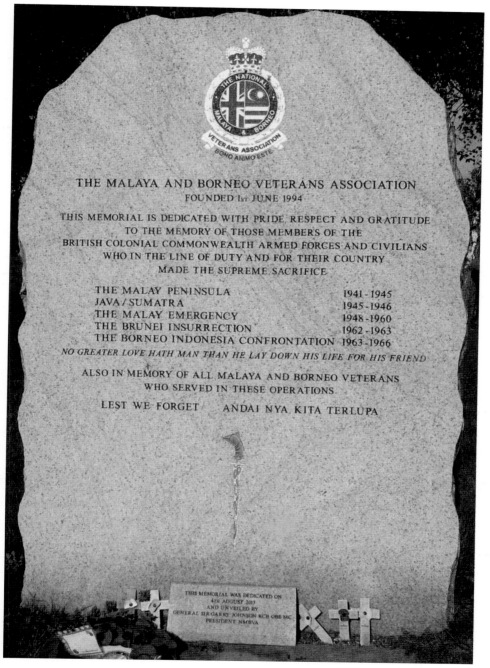

Malaya and Borneo Veterans' Association Memorial at the National Memorial Arboretum in England. (Photo Gerry van Tonder)

However, this patrolling plus an intense propaganda effort of leaflet airdrop and radio programmes, plus RAF and RAAF bombing using, in my time, Avro Lancastrians to Short Sunderlands; RAN and RAAF helicopter reconnaissance and transport support; fixed wing Auster reconnaissance; aerial photography; artillery shelling; and being spied upon by police informers, would have been acutely stressful to the CT.

All coordinated together by Malaya Command to deprive the CT of contact with their Min Yuen support and refuge in their jungle sanctuaries. This ultimately deprived them of their ability to move freely and terrorise the civilian population. So they withered slowly on their unsustained vine.

Peaceful surrender became a better option to a slowly eroding cause than deprivation and death. So the CT and the 'Emergency' fizzled out, leaving a tiny hard-core element, with Chin Peng, hiding in neutral Thailand.

I left Malaya having had 516 humid, sweaty and physically demanding days and nights during which I and my askari platoon of the Rhodesian African Rifles had been on operations in the *ulu*, swamps, mangroves and mountains, and walked and patrolled at least one thousand miles. During which we had nine contacts, three successful, with the CT. In fact, they were better at avoiding us than we were in finding them. However, in the strategy of denial the overwhelming British-led security forces had bested them. The 'indirect approach' strategy with minimum SF casualties had won.

Strategically, one would think the UK were the winners, but this should be tempered by at what cost, financially? Or to what purpose, economically: because Malaya after *Merdeka* [Malayan for independent or free] was no longer a UK economic domain. Also, to what aim internationally or internally in the UK? Chinese hegemony was thwarted. Singapore, under Lee Kuan Yew, was unshackled and boomed. Indonesia became over-confident and stroppy and caused more UK and Australian military involvement. FARELF scuttled temporarily into a puny token force into Hong Kong. Sarawak became independent.

The British Empire shrunk further. The UK, the lesson learnt, sensibly stayed out of Vietnam. The Brits fell into the EU via the Common Market, and concentrated on NATO. The UK military shrank into a paper-thin tiger, unready but angry for the Falklands. The Empire disappeared.

The UK economy floundered. So who won? If you believe in my trickle downwards of well-interspersed falling dominos above, not the UK, economically or militarily, in the long term. However, China's hegemony was significantly arrested.

The British security forces defeated the Communists who created the 'Emergency', but damaged themselves in so doing.

Immediate winners were the British. Immediate losers were the Communist Terrorists of the MRLA and their China supporters.

The costs of the Emergency between 1948 to 1955 were US$200 million a year for the Malay Government and US$500 million per year for the UK government.

So, take your pick! Short term, or long term?

I had been shot at and shot back to kill, so it seemed to me and my men that we had been in a war. Later I found out that it was titled an 'emergency' so that the rubber and tin industries could claim against Lloyds insurers, something that they would not have been able to do if it had been declared a 'war'. This was political dissembling and devious capitalism at its very best.

An RAF Pioneer being unloaded. (Courtesy Rhodesian African Rifles Regimental Association (UK))

SELECTED BIBLIOGRAPHY

Books

Essex-Clark, Brigadier John, *Maverick Soldier: An Infantryman's Story* (Melbourne University Press, Australia, 2014)

Pittaway, Jonathan, *Special Air Service: The Men Speak* (Dandy Agencies, South Africa, 2009)

Templer, General Sir Gerald, *The Conduct of Anti-Terrorist Operations in Malaya* (Produced by the High Commissioner and Director of Operations, 1958 edition)

Academic and Archived Military Papers

Binda, Alexandre, *Masodja: The History of the Rhodesian African Rifles and its forerunner the Rhodesian Native Regiment* (30 Degrees South Publishing, South Africa, 2007)

Drabble, John H., *Economic History of Malaysia* (University of Sydney lecture, Australia)

Ling, Dr Ho Hui, *The Rubber and Tin Industries in Malaya During The Emergency, 1948–1960* (History Department lecture, University of Malaya, 2006)

Morton, J.P., *The Problems We Faced in Malaya and How They Were Solved* (lecture notes, July 1954, 16th Security Service release, National Archives, 2007)

Nicholls, Lt Col C.R., *Salient Features of Patrols and Ambushes in the Malayan Emergency* (memorandum 1/53, Operational Research Section)

ACKNOWLEDGEMENTS

I extend my sincere gratitude and that of the production team to Colonel Dudley Wall for his untiring work in providing us with the magnificent, detailed colour images.

To Brigadier 'Digger' Essex-Clark for invaluable first-hand accounts and views of active combat in Malaya during the emergency.

To my good friend and former RhAR officer during the Rhodesian terrorist war of the 1970s, Russell Fulton: grateful thanks for the captivating portrait of Warrant Officer Pisayi Muzerecho.

This publication has been enriched with the remarkable personal interviews I was privileged to have had with two old gentlemen who experienced Malaya, both who also generously shared their own photographs. My heartfelt thanks to John Anderson and Frank Walker for taking me on their Malayan journeys. These two interviews were facilitated by two good friends – sisters Laura Kirkman and Sharron Arrowsmith. Sadly, John Anderson passed away on 20 February 2017, a few days before this book was sent to print. He will be deeply missed.

For providing me with photographs and written material, Craig Fourie, Jonathan Pittaway and the Rhodesian African Rifles Regimental Association (UK).

HRH Queen Elizabeth the Queen Mother inspects soldiers of the RhAR. (Courtesy Rhodesian African Rifles Regimental Association (UK))

ABOUT THE AUTHOR

Born and raised in Southern Rhodesia, fulltime historian, researcher, copy-editor and published author, Gerry van Tonder came to Britain in 1999, settling in Derby, the city of his wife Tracey's birth. In Rhodesia, he completed 18 months' national conscription during the guerrilla war of the 1970s, before reading for a Bachelor of Administration (Honours) degree at the University of Rhodesia. He served as a Liaison and Returning Officer during the Zimbabwean elections of 1980.

Gerry has co-authored *Rhodesian Combined Forces Roll of Honour 1966–1981*, the landmark definitive *Rhodesia Regiment 1899–1981* (a copy of this book was presented to the regiment's former colonel-in-chief, Her Majesty the Queen) and authored *Rhodesian Native Regiment/Rhodesian African Rifles Book of Remembrance*. He has just completed the co-authored *North of the Red Line: Recollections of the Border War by Members of the SADF and SWATF 1966–1989*, released in July 2016. He is also working on a further Rhodesian title, *Operation Lighthouse*, an account of the role of a para-military government ministry in the 1970s guerrilla insurgency. He has written three local history books: *Derby in 50 Buildings*, *Chesterfield's Military Heritage* and *Mansfield Through Time*. This is his second Cold War title for Pen & Sword, after *Berlin Blockade: Soviet Chokehold and the Great Allied Airlift 1948–49*. Gerry has his own website: www.rhodesiansoldier.com

The author and Platoon Warrant Officer Pisayi Muzerecho MM, meet at the National Memorial Arboretum in England in June 2015. (Courtesy Andries van Tonder)